Discover the pleasures of fabulous, satisfying food...

Designed to make eating healthily enjoyable and sustainable, *Seriously Satisfying* has 130 delicious recipes, ranging from fabulously filling breakfasts and brunches to mouth-watering desserts.

Seriously Satisfying has something for everyone and every occasion. There's a fantastic selection of favourites to choose from for the family or simply just for you. To impress your friends and family with incredibly delicious recipes, turn to the chocolate chapter. And whether you're looking for a light meal, a satisfying soup or something fast, you'll be spoilt for choice.

Throughout the book, you'll find helpful Cook's tips and, at the start of each chapter, there's an index listing the recipes in order of timings so, at a glance, you can find the quickest recipes more easily and plan ahead for dishes that take longer. All the recipes are easy to follow, with clear step-by-step instructions, enabling both new and experienced cooks to discover some favourite dishes.

With so many fresh ideas to choose from, you'll have all the inspiration you need to create delicious meals everyone will love.

...for breakfast, lunch and supper, you'll be spoilt for choice

great starts
to the day

Whether you're looking for a delicious way to start the day or for something a bit different for brunch, you won't be disappointed with these tasty and satisfying ideas. They'll get you going and give you the fantastic start you need. Grab a fast and filling Oaty Apricot Smoothie or pack up a delicious slice of Banana Loaf to take to work. And for a more leisurely weekend brunch, enjoy a slice of Herby French Toast or a sensational Sausage Omelette.

One pan ham 'n' egg on toast on page 8

One pan ham 'n' egg on toast

Calories per serving 263
Takes 10 mins

Serves 1

Quick and easy, with only one pan to wash up.

low fat cooking spray
1 slice wholemeal bread
1 egg
2 Parma ham slices
½ teaspoon snipped fresh chives, to garnish
(optional)
1 tablespoon tomato ketchup, to serve

1 Spray a non stick frying pan with the cooking spray and heat until hot. Add the bread, placing it to one side of the pan.
2 Crack the egg into a ramekin or cup and carefully add to the pan. Cook for 2–3 minutes until the white is set or cooked to your liking.
3 Meanwhile, turn the bread over after a minute or so, when the underside is brown. Add the Parma ham to the pan and cook for 1–2 minutes until crispy, turning once.
4 Slide everything from the pan on to a warmed serving plate and serve garnished with chives (if using) and the tomato ketchup on the side.

Try this Serve your breakfast with two rashers of extra lean back bacon instead of the Parma ham.

Honey citrus crêpes

Calories per serving 294
Takes 25 mins
V **for pancakes only**

Serves 4

Perfect for a wake up brunch at the weekend and great with half a sliced banana added to each plate.

125 g (4½ oz) plain flour
1 egg
300 ml (10 fl oz) skimmed milk
3 oranges
2 grapefruits
2 tablespoons runny honey
low fat cooking spray

1 Place the flour in a mixing bowl and make a well in the middle. Break in the egg and using a wooden spoon, begin stirring, gently drawing in the flour. Once too stiff to mix, add a little milk and mix well. Continue stirring until all the milk is added and the batter is smooth. Finely grate the zest of one of the oranges and stir into the batter. Leave to stand for 5 minutes.
2 Cut the skin away from all of the fruit removing any white pith. Carefully cut between the segments letting the pieces and any juice collect in a bowl. Stir in the honey.
3 Spray a medium sized, non stick frying pan with the cooking spray and heat until hot. Add a ladleful of batter, swirling round the pan to the edges. Cook for about a minute until brown underneath and then carefully loosen the edges and flip over to cook the other side. Slide from the pan and keep warm by covering with foil while you cook the other seven crêpes.
4 Serve two crêpes each, with the fruits and honeyed juices divided between the plates.

Sausage and mushroom sarnie

Calories per serving 191
Takes 15 mins

Serves 2

A satisfying meal for breakfast, brunch or lunch.

2 low fat thick pork sausages (such as Weight Watchers
   Premium Pork Sausages)
2 large or 4 medium field mushrooms
low fat cooking spray
4 slices low calorie bread
a drizzle of Worcestershire sauce

1 Preheat the grill to medium. Line the grill pan with foil and grill the sausages for 4 minutes, turning once. Add the mushrooms to the pan, spray with the cooking spray and cook for another 6–8 minutes, turning once until soft and juicy. Turn the sausages again so they brown all over.

2 Meanwhile, toast the bread. To assemble, top two slices of toast with the mushrooms and drizzle over the Worcestershire sauce. Cut the sausages in half lengthways, place on top of the mushrooms and sandwich with the other slices of toast. Serve immediately.

Try this Serve each sarnie with 1 tablespoon of tomato ketchup.

Summer fruits porridge

Calories per serving 241
Takes 10 mins

Serves 2

Although porridge is generally thought of more as a winter breakfast, adding a good portion of summer fruits makes it a delicious option in the warmer months too.

300 ml (10 fl oz) skimmed milk
110 g (4 oz) frozen summer fruits
25 g (1 oz) soft brown sugar
70 g (2½ oz) porridge oats

1 In a jug, mix the milk with 100 ml (3½ fl oz) cold water.

2 Place the frozen summer fruits in a small pan with the sugar and cook over a gentle heat, stirring occasionally, for 3–5 minutes until softened and the juices begin to run.

3 Meanwhile, place the oats and milk in another pan and cook gently, stirring regularly, for 3–5 minutes until thickened and hot.

4 Serve two bowls of porridge with the summer fruits spooned over.

Sausage omelette

Calories per serving 237   Serves 2
Takes 20 mins

low fat cooking spray
2 low fat thick sausages (such as Weight Watchers
    Premium Pork Sausages), each chopped into
    four pieces
3 eggs, beaten
2 tablespoons chopped fresh curly parsley
freshly ground black pepper

1   Spray a non stick frying pan with the cooking spray
and heat until hot. Add the sausage pieces and cook,
stirring occasionally, until brown and cooked through.

2   Season the eggs with black pepper and stir in the
parsley. Add to the pan, with the sausages, swirling round
to the edges. Cook the omelette for about 2 minutes,
lifting the cooked edges, and tipping any uncooked
egg underneath.

3   Once all the egg is set and the underneath is cooked,
slice into wedges and serve.

Try this Use four rashers of lean back bacon, pan fried
for 3–4 minutes in step 1 and then chopped, instead of
the sausages.

Oaty apricot smoothie

Calories per serving 169   Serves 1
Takes 5 mins

Whizz up a smoothie to enjoy a quick and filling breakfast.

15 g (½ oz) porridge oats
½ × 411 g can apricots in natural juice, drained
200 ml (7 fl oz) skimmed milk

1   Place the oats in a small frying pan and heat until hot.
Move around the pan until golden, but make sure they
don't burn. Set aside to cool slightly.

2   Place the oats, apricots and milk in a liquidiser, or
use a hand held blender, and whizz until smooth. Serve
immediately.

Banana loaf

Calories per serving 193
20 mins prep, 1 hr cooking

This moist and flavoursome wholemeal loaf freezes well.
Serve with a tablespoon of 0% fat Greek yogurt per slice.

low fat cooking spray
400 g (14 oz) bananas
finely grated zest and juice of a lime
200 g (7 oz) wholemeal self raising flour
½ teaspoon mixed spice
75 g (2¾ oz) low fat spread
110 g (4 oz) light brown sugar
2 eggs, beaten
½ teaspoon runny honey

You will need a 900 g (2 lb) loaf tin; non stick
baking parchment

1 Preheat the oven to Gas Mark 4/180°C/fan oven 160°C.
Line the base of the loaf tin with the baking parchment and
spray with the cooking spray.
2 Mash the bananas with the lime zest and juice and set
aside. Sift the flour and spice into a mixing bowl, adding
any bran left in the sieve and rub in the low fat spread with
your fingers until well combined. Stir in the sugar.
3 Stir the banana mixture and the beaten eggs into the
flour until smooth, then spoon into the prepared tin. Bake
for 1 hour or until an inserted skewer comes out clean.
Drizzle over the honey. Leave to cool in the tin. Once cool,
store in an airtight container for 3 days or slice and freeze.

cook's tip...

Wholemeal flour adds a slightly nutty flavour but
white flour works equally well.

Herby French toasts

Calories per serving 151	Serves 4
Takes 15 mins	

A great way to use up slightly stale bread.

450 g (1 lb) tomatoes on the vine, chopped roughly
1 teaspoon balsamic vinegar
½ teaspoon brown sugar
1 egg, beaten
100 ml (3½ fl oz) skimmed milk
2 teaspoons fresh thyme leaves
low fat cooking spray
4 medium slices bread
freshly ground black pepper

1 Place the tomatoes in a small lidded pan with the vinegar and sugar. Bring to the boil, cover and gently simmer for 5–10 minutes until pulpy.

2 Beat together the egg and milk in a shallow bowl and stir in the thyme with some black pepper. Spray a non stick frying pan with the cooking spray and heat until hot. Dip each slice of bread in the egg mixture covering both sides and add to the pan. Cook for 2–3 minutes until golden on both sides, turning once.

3 Serve a slice of toast each with the tomatoes spooned on the side.

Try this Add 1 slice of lean back bacon per person.

Cinnamon peach twists

Calories per serving 219	Makes 6
20 mins prep + 30 mins proving, 15 mins cooking	

Serve with 75 g (2¾ oz) 0% fat Greek yogurt per person.

300 g (10½ oz) strong white bread flour,
1 tablespoon reserved
7 g sachet instant yeast
3 tablespoons light brown sugar
low fat cooking spray
411 g can peach halves in natural juice,
drained, with 1 tablespoon juice reserved
1 teaspoon cinnamon

1 Sift the flour into a large bowl and stir in the yeast and 2 tablespoons of the sugar. Make a well in the middle and add 150–175 ml (5–6 fl oz) hand hot water. Use a wooden spoon to draw in the flour to make a dough. Once it is too stiff to mix, use your hands to bring the dough together.

2 Sift the reserved flour over a clean work surface. Knead the dough for 5 minutes until smooth and stretchy. Return it to the bowl, cover with a tea towel and leave in a warm place to rise, until doubled in size – about 30 minutes.

3 Preheat the oven to Gas Mark 7/220°C/fan oven 200°C. Spray a baking tray with the cooking spray.

4 Remove the dough from the bowl and knead it lightly. Divide into six pieces. Roll each piece into a rectangle, approximately 12 x 8 cm (4½ x 3¼ inches).

5 Place a peach half in the middle, then twist the ends, dabbing them with a little peach juice to help them stick and keep the fruit in place. The peach should be visible in the middle. Transfer to the baking tray. Repeat with all the pieces of dough. Brush over the reserved juice.

6 Mix together the remaining sugar and cinnamon. Sprinkle over the twists. Bake for 15 minutes until golden and puffed up. Serve warm.

Sweetcorn and tomato cheesy muffins

Calories per serving 140	**Makes 12**
10 mins prep, 15 mins cooking	

Enjoy these tasty muffins with a crisp green apple, cut into wedges, on the side.

60 g (2 oz) sun-dried tomatoes
3 tablespoons boiling water
225 g (8 oz) self raising flour
2 teaspoons baking powder
a pinch of salt
2 teaspoons dried thyme
200 g (7 oz) frozen sweetcorn, defrosted
60 g (2 oz) reduced fat Cheddar cheese, grated
1 egg, beaten
200 ml (7 fl oz) skimmed milk
2 tablespoons vegetable oil

You will need a muffin tin; 12 muffin cases

1 Soak the tomatoes in the boiling water for 10 minutes.
2 Preheat the oven to Gas Mark 6/200°C/fan oven 180°C. Line the muffin tin with the muffin cases.
3 Drain the tomatoes, reserving the liquid, and chop them into pieces.
4 Sift the flour, baking powder and salt into a large bowl, then stir in the thyme, sweetcorn, cheese and chopped tomatoes.
5 In a jug, beat together the egg, milk, oil and reserved soaking liquid. Make a well in the middle of the flour and add the wet ingredients. Stir to combine (don't worry if it is lumpy) and spoon into the cases. Bake for 12–15 minutes until golden. Cool in the tray for 5 minutes. Serve warm or cool completely on a wire rack.

Try this Serve each muffin with a tablespoon of ketchup.

To freeze, cool and place in a freezerproof container. To serve, defrost thoroughly and warm through for about 30 seconds in a microwave or 5–10 minutes in a moderate oven.

Although these muffins taste best if eaten the same day, they can be kept in an airtight container for 2–3 days. Refresh in a warm oven for 5 minutes before eating.

Spinach and smoked haddock

Calories per serving 215 **Serves 2**
Takes 15 mins

Serve with a 50 g (1¾ oz) wedge of soda bread per person.

180 g (6 oz) cherry tomatoes on the vine
**   (about 2 vines)**
150 ml (5 fl oz) skimmed milk
2 × 175 g (6 oz) smoked haddock fillet
1 bay leaf
200 g bag spinach leaves, rinsed
freshly ground black pepper

You will need a large shallow lidded pan

1 Preheat the grill to medium and place the tomatoes, vine side down, on the grill pan. Cook for 5–6 minutes until softened and beginning to char.

2 Meanwhile, pour the milk into the shallow lidded pan with the fish, skin side down, and the bay leaf. Bring to the boil, cover and simmer for 5 minutes until just cooked; it should flake easily. Remove the fish from the pan with a slotted spoon, leaving the milk in the pan, and set aside. Cover with foil to keep warm.

3 Add the spinach to the pan with the milk, bring back to the boil, stirring the spinach until it just wilts. This will only take a minute. Season with black pepper.

4 To serve, spoon the spinach on to warm plates, add a fillet of fish and put the tomatoes alongside. Drizzle over the remaining milk. Season with black pepper and serve immediately.

On the weekend, take the time to savour and enjoy this delicious, traditional brunch.

lunches + light meals

Does lunch feel a bit repetitive these days? Do you need some inspiration? Then look no further – we've come up with some great new combinations to jazz up your midday meals. The Salmon Pâté Bagel is ideal for lunch on the go or for a change, you might like to try some delicious Roasted Beetroot with Fennel and Orange. If you're sharing lunch with friends, they'll love the Lamb Falafel and for a lighter meal, you can choose from quick and easy options such as Baked Eggs and Tomatoes or Mushroom Bruschetta flavoured with thyme.

Red pepper and cheese tarts on page 30

Griddled smoky chicken with potato salad

Calories per serving 317　　　　　**Serves 4**
20 mins prep, 25 mins cooking
✻ chicken only

Smoked paprika's lovely flavour goes well with most meats. Serve with a green salad of cucumber and Little Gem lettuce.

500 g (1 lb 2 oz) new potatoes, halved if large
200 g (7 oz) green beans, trimmed
**　　and chopped into 5 cm (2 inch) pieces**
4 spring onions, chopped
8 cherry tomatoes, halved
2 tablespoons reduced fat mayonnaise
4 × 150 g (5½ oz) skinless, boneless
**　　chicken breasts**
1½ tablespoons smoked paprika
low fat cooking spray
salt and freshly ground black pepper

1 Bring a lidded pan of water to the boil. Add the potatoes, cover and cook for 10 minutes. Add the beans and cook for another 13–15 minutes. Drain thoroughly and stir in the spring onions, tomatoes and mayonnaise. Season with black pepper.

2 Meanwhile, place the chicken breasts on a board between two sheets of cling film and flatten with the end of a rolling pin until 5 mm (¼ inch) thick. Remove the top sheet of cling film, dust the topside with half of the paprika and season.

3 Heat a griddle or non stick frying pan until hot. Spray the dusted side of the chicken with the cooking spray and place that side down on the hot pan. Cook for 3–4 minutes until browned on the underside. Dust the top side with the remaining paprika and spray with the cooking spray. Turn the chicken over and cook the other side for 2–3 minutes until golden. You may need to do this in batches. Serve the chicken with the potato salad on the side.

Soba noodles with wasabi beef

Calories per serving 326	Serves 4
Takes 15 mins	

This filling and tasty Japanese-style stir fry is ideal for a quick midweek lunch.

170 g (6 oz) dried soba noodles
400 g (14 oz) thin cut lean sirloin steaks, visible
    fat removed
2 teaspoons wasabi paste, plus 2 teaspoons to serve
low fat cooking spray
1 yellow or red pepper, de-seeded and chopped
200 g (7 oz) sugar snap peas
3 tablespoons light soy sauce
salt

1 Bring a large pan of water to the boil, add the noodles, bring back to the boil and cook for 5–7 minutes, or according to the packet instructions. Drain well and keep warm.

2 Meanwhile, season each steak with a little salt and spread the wasabi paste over each before cutting into thin strips.

3 Spray a large wok or non stick frying pan with the cooking spray and heat until hot. Add the beef, peppers and sugar snap peas. Cook over a high heat, stirring for 2–4 minutes until the beef is cooked to your liking.

4 Toss the noodles in the soy sauce and serve with the beef and vegetables and, if you wish, the extra wasabi.

Grilled vegetable tostadas

Calories per serving 366	Serves 2
10 mins prep, 15 mins cooking	

Grilling is a great way to cook vegetables. It creates a lovely, light charring and the vegetables retain a delicious bite. If you like spice, serve with a teaspoon of hot chilli sauce per person.

1 large courgette, trimmed and sliced
1 red onion, sliced thinly
1 red pepper, de-seeded and chopped
2 tomatoes on the vine, quartered
low fat cooking spray
2 × 60 g (2 oz) tortilla wraps
40 g (1½ oz) wafer thin ham, shredded
25 g (1 oz) half fat mature Cheddar cheese, grated

1 Preheat the grill to medium. Line the grill pan with foil and arrange all the vegetables on the pan so they sit on one level. Spray liberally with the cooking spray. Grill for 5 minutes then turn and cook for another 5 minutes.

2 Remove the foil and vegetables from the tray. Lay the wraps on the grill pan (you may have to do this one at a time), divide the vegetables, ham and cheese between them and grill for 2–3 minutes until the cheese is melted and the tortilla is warm. Serve immediately.

cook's tip...

Instead of buying a large pack you may not be able to use up, buy the wafer thin ham at the deli counter.

Roasted beetroot with fennel and orange

Calories per serving 154   Serves 2
10 mins prep, 20 mins cooking

Serve with a 50 g (1¾ oz) wedge of fresh wholemeal bread per person.

140 g (5 oz) beetroot, unpeeled and
    sliced into thin wedges
1 yellow pepper, de-seeded and sliced
1 teaspoon extra virgin olive oil
1 orange
1 fennel bulb, sliced thinly
2 teaspoons balsamic vinegar
30 g (1¼ oz) light feta cheese

You will need a small roasting tin

1 Preheat the oven to Gas Mark 6/200°C/fan oven 180°C. Place the beetroot and pepper in the roasting tin, drizzle over the olive oil and roast for 20 minutes until softened and beginning to char.

2 Meanwhile, using a sharp knife, cut away the orange peel then cut between the pith lines to segment the orange. Do this over a bowl to collect any juices. Arrange the orange segments and fennel slices on two serving plates. Top with the hot beetroot and peppers.

3 Stir the orange juice and balsamic vinegar into the roasting tin, scraping up any sticky bits, then spoon over the salad. Crumble the cheese over the top and serve.

Slice the beetroot wedges quite thinly so they cook quickly but still retain some bite.

Red pepper and cheese tarts

Calories per serving 222	**Serves 4**
15 mins prep, 15 mins cooking	

2 red peppers, halved and de-seeded
4 × 45 g (1½ oz) sheets filo pastry, measuring
    50 × 24 cm (20 × 9½ inches), defrosted if frozen
low fat cooking spray
2 teaspoons balsamic vinegar
2 teaspoons fresh thyme leaves
75 g (2¾ oz) rinded goat's cheese, sliced into 4 rounds
100 g (3½ oz) rocket leaves, to serve
freshly ground black pepper

You will need a four hole Yorkshire pudding tin

1 Preheat the grill to high and cook the peppers, skin side up, for about 5 minutes until the skin begins to blacken. Place in a plastic bag for 5 minutes to help release the skins.
2 Preheat the oven to Gas Mark 6/200°C/fan oven 180°C. Cut each sheet of filo into four rectangles. Spray each with the cooking spray and use to line the four holes of the Yorkshire pudding tin. Layer the pieces at angles so you cover the hole completely with the corners sticking out.
3 Peel the skin from the peppers and discard. Slice the flesh thinly. Toss each pepper with the balsamic vinegar, thyme leaves and season with black pepper. Spoon into the pastry cases and top with the cheese rounds. Bake for 10–15 minutes until the pastry is golden and the cheese has melted. Serve with the rocket leaves.

> ❄ **To freeze, carefully place the tarts in a freezerproof container (the pastry is quite fragile). To serve, defrost and warm through in the oven for 5–10 minutes at Gas Mark 4/180°C/fan oven 160°C.**

Salmon pâté bagels

Calories per serving 322	**Serves 2**
Takes 10 mins	

For extra crunch add half a diced red pepper to the mixture.

180 g can red salmon
10 cm (4 inch) cucumber, diced
finely grated zest of ½ a lemon, plus wedges
2 tablespoons chopped fresh dill
1 tablespoon 0% fat Greek yogurt
2 × 70 g (2½ oz) low fat bagels, split
freshly ground black pepper

1 Preheat the grill to medium. Place the salmon in a small bowl and mash with a fork. Stir in the cucumber, lemon zest, dill and yogurt and season with black pepper.
2 Place the bagel halves on the grill pan, cut side up, and toast until golden. Remove from the grill and divide the salmon mixture between the bagel halves; there should be enough to cover all four pieces. Serve with lemon wedges to squeeze over.

Try this If you're not keen on the light aniseed flavour of dill, use chopped fresh curly parsley instead.

Tuna and bean pasta salad

Calories per serving 379	Serves 1
Takes 20 mins	
❄ tuna only	

Serve with a generous handful of rocket and halved cherry tomatoes.

50 g (1¾ oz) dried pasta shapes, such as fusilli
25 g (1 oz) green beans, trimmed and chopped
100 g (3½ oz) fresh tuna steaks
low fat cooking spray
1 teaspoon sesame seeds
1 tablespoon 0% fat Greek yogurt
25 g (1 oz) canned sweetcorn, drained
salt and freshly ground black pepper

1 Bring a small pan of water to the boil, add the pasta and cook according to the packet instructions, adding the beans for the final 3 minutes of cooking time. Drain and return to the pan.

2 Heat a non stick frying pan until hot. Spray the tuna with the cooking spray on both sides and season. Cook for 1–2 minutes on one side, until just beginning to brown. Sprinkle the sesame seeds over the top of the uncooked side, pressing them into the flesh. Then turn over the tuna and cook on the other side for a further minute.

3 Stir the yogurt and sweetcorn into the pasta and beans, season with black pepper and serve on the side with the tuna.

Smoked mackerel and couscous salad

Calories per serving 435	Serves 1
Takes 15 mins	
❄ mackerel only	

Smoked mackerel has quite a strong flavour so a little goes a long way. You may like to buy the required amount from the fish counter or, if you buy a pack, freeze any remaining mackerel for another time.

1 orange
40 g (1½ oz) couscous
10 cm (4 inch) cucumber, diced
2 spring onions, chopped
1 small carrot, peeled and grated
55 g (1¾ oz) skinless smoked mackerel fillet
a handful of watercress

1 Finely grate the zest from half the orange into a bowl and mix in the couscous. Squeeze the juice from that orange half – it should be about 3 tablespoons. Add another tablespoon or two of water to the juice. Pour over the couscous and leave to soak for 10 minutes, until all the liquid has been absorbed.

2 Peel and chop the remaining orange half.

3 Fluff the couscous with a fork to separate the grains then stir in the orange pieces, cucumber, spring onions and carrot. Flake the mackerel into chunks and serve on top of the couscous with the watercress on the side.

cook's tip...

If packing this for a lunchbox, keep the watercress separate or put it on top of the couscous loosely, otherwise it will wilt.

Leek and potato rosti bake

> **Calories per serving 138**   Serves 4
> 10 mins prep, 35 mins cooking
>

A quick and simple way to make a delicious rosti.

low fat cooking spray
450 g (1 lb) floury potatoes (such as Maris Piper or King Edward), peeled
2 leeks, trimmed and shredded finely
2 teaspoons mixed dried herbs
60 g (2 oz) reduced fat Brie, sliced
salt and freshly ground black pepper

To serve
100 g bag mixed green leaves
2 tablespoons balsamic vinegar

You will need a 20 cm (8 inch) springform tin; non stick baking parchment

1 Preheat the oven to Gas Mark 6/200°C/fan oven 180°C. Line the base of the tin with the baking parchment and spray the sides with the cooking spray.

2 Coarsely grate the potatoes, place in a clean tea towel and squeeze out any excess liquid. Transfer to a bowl. Mix in the leeks and herbs and season. Press the mixture into the prepared tin and bake for 20–25 minutes until golden.

3 Remove from the oven and scatter over the Brie, giving it a minute to melt before removing the rosti from the tin. Cut into slices and serve warm with the green leaves and balsamic vinegar.

> To save time, you can grate the potatoes in a food processor.

Mushroom bruschetta

> **Calories per serving 175**   Serves 1
> Takes 15 mins
>

Serve topped with 10 g (¼ oz) freshly grated Parmesan cheese.

low fat cooking spray
150 g (5½ oz) mushrooms, sliced
2 spring onions, sliced
1 teaspoon fresh thyme leaves
2 × 20 g (¾ oz) baguette slices
1 garlic clove, halved
1 teaspoon extra virgin olive oil

1 Preheat the grill to medium. Spray a small non stick frying pan with the cooking spray and heat until hot. Add the mushrooms, spring onions and thyme and stir fry for about 5 minutes until the mushrooms have released their juices.

2 Place the baguette slices on the grill pan and grill on both sides until golden. Rub the cut side of the garlic over the toast to flavour it and then discard the garlic. Drizzle the olive oil over the toast and top with the hot mushrooms. Serve immediately.

Lamb falafel

Calories per serving 329　　　　　　**Serves 4**
10 mins prep, 8 mins cooking
⊛ **falafel only**

Serve with soft round lettuce, sliced tomatoes and a 15 cm (6 inch) piece of cucumber, chopped.

½ × 400 g can chick peas, drained
200 g (7 oz) lean lamb mince
½ teaspoon ground coriander
½ teaspoon ground cumin
low fat cooking spray
4 × 60 g (2 oz) soft tortilla wraps
4 tablespoons 0% fat Greek yogurt
2 teaspoons chopped fresh mint
salt and freshly ground black pepper

1 Place the chick peas in a mixing bowl and roughly mash them with a potato masher or fork. Mix in the lamb and spices and season. It is easier to mix this with your hands. Shape the mixture into 12 walnut size balls.

2 Preheat the grill to medium. Spray a non stick frying pan with the cooking spray and heat until hot. Fry the falafel for 5–8 minutes, turning regularly to brown all over. Meanwhile, warm the wraps under the preheated grill for a couple of minutes.

3 Mix the yogurt and mint together with some black pepper. To serve, place three falafel in the middle of each wrap, add a tablespoon of yogurt to each and fold up to a cone. Serve with the salad alongside.

Try this Lamb is a traditional Middle Eastern meat but these falafel are also delicious with chicken mince.

cook's tips...

You can heat the wraps in the microwave for a few seconds instead of heating them under the grill.

Store the other half of the can of chick peas in a plastic airtight container in the fridge for 3 days.

Deliciously spiced Middle Eastern meatballs are ideal for lunch or a light meal.

Toasted aubergine dip

Serve this dip with two carrots, a red pepper and a celery stick, cut into batons.

2 aubergines, about 200 g (7 oz) each
finely grated zest and juice of a lemon
1 garlic clove, crushed
25 g (1 oz) low fat soft cheese
2 tablespoons roughly chopped fresh parsley
4 × 55 g (1¾ oz) pitta breads
2 teaspoons extra virgin olive oil
salt and freshly ground black pepper

1   Preheat the grill to medium. Grill the aubergines, turning regularly for about 10 minutes until the skin is charred and quite soft. Remove from the grill and once cool enough to handle, peel away the skin. Roughly chop the flesh and place in a food processor.

2   Blend the aubergines briefly, then add the lemon zest and juice and garlic. Blend again before adding the cheese and parsley. Taste and season accordingly. Leave to cool.

3   Put the pitta on a grill pan and grill on both sides until toasted. Cut into strips.

4   Drizzle the olive oil over the aubergine mixture and serve with the toasted pitta bread strips.

Baked eggs and tomatoes

Calories per serving 253   Serves 4
5 mins prep, 25 mins cooking
V

An easy but very tasty and satisfying lunch or supper.

900 g (2 lb) tomatoes on the vine, halved
1 teaspoon dried thyme
25 g (1 oz) low fat spread
4 eggs
salt and freshly ground black pepper
4 × 40 g (1½ oz) slices white crusty bread, to serve

1   Preheat the oven to Gas Mark 6/200°C/fan oven 180°C. Lay the tomatoes in an ovenproof dish, cut side up, so they sit together snugly. Sprinkle over the thyme, season and then dot with the low fat spread. Bake for 15 minutes until beginning to soften.

2   Remove from the oven and make four wells between the tomatoes. Crack an egg into each well and return to the oven for 10 minutes.

3   Season with black pepper and serve hot with the bread for mopping up the juices.

V **Try this**   Instead of bread, this is also delicious with a jacket potato. Place four 110 g (4 oz) scrubbed potatoes in the oven for 20 minutes before the tomatoes go in, cooking for 40–50 minutes in total until cooked through.

love soup

Comforting and filling, soup is easy to love. And when you add a tasty twist to classic recipes, they sometimes taste even better: see what we mean when you enjoy a warming bowl of Beef Minestrone with Horseradish Sauce or Leek and Potato Soup with crispy Parma ham. There are some lovely Asian-style soups too: choose from Miso Bean Soup or the spicy Tom Yam Soup from Thailand.

French onion soup with toasts on page 46

Lettuce and pea soup

Calories per serving 67	Serves 2
Takes 25 mins	

This is a great summer soup, especially if there is a lot of lettuce from the garden to use up. Serve with a 55 g (1¾ oz) toasted pitta bread each.

low fat cooking spray
4 spring onions, sliced
250 g (9 oz) lettuce, such as Cos or Little Gem, shredded
150 ml (5 fl oz) vegetable stock
100 ml (3½ fl oz) skimmed milk
60 g (2 oz) peas, fresh or frozen
4 fresh mint leaves, shredded, plus extra to garnish
freshly ground black pepper

1 Spray a large lidded pan with the cooking spray and heat until hot. Add the spring onions and stir fry for about 3 minutes until softened. Add the lettuce and cook for a minute before stirring in the stock and milk.

2 Bring to the boil, add the peas and reduce the heat to a steady simmer. Cover and cook for 5 minutes.

3 Stir in the shredded mint then transfer to a liquidiser to blend or whizz with a hand held blender. Season with a little black pepper and return to the pan to warm through.

4 Serve in warm bowls garnished with the mint leaves.

Tomato, plum and basil soup

Calories per serving 142	Serves 2
10 mins prep, 30 mins cooking	

Plums add a terrific tang to this easy soup.

300 g (10½ oz) tomatoes on the vine, vine removed, and halved
2 garlic cloves, unpeeled and left whole
300 g (10½ oz) plums, halved and stoned
low fat cooking spray
500 ml (18 fl oz) vegetable stock
50 g (1¾ oz) low fat soft cheese
a large handful of fresh basil leaves, shredded
salt and freshly ground black pepper

1 Preheat the oven to Gas Mark 6/200°C/fan oven 180°C. Place the tomatoes, garlic and plums in a large roasting tray and spray with the cooking spray. Toss to coat and cook for 30 minutes until soft and oozing.

2 Remove the garlic cloves and squeeze the flesh from their skins. Put the contents of the roasting tin, including the garlic flesh in a large pan, scraping in any caramelised bits from the tin and then pour in the stock.

3 Add the soft cheese and blend with a hand held blender until smooth. Alternatively, transfer to a liquidiser to blend and then return to the pan. Warm through until hot, season to taste and stir through the basil just before serving.

Beef minestrone with horseradish sauce

Calories per serving 181   Serves 4
15 mins prep, 15 mins cooking
❄ soup only

A deliciously hearty main meal soup.

low fat cooking spray
2 celery sticks, chopped
1 large onion, chopped
1 green pepper, de-seeded and chopped
2 garlic cloves, crushed
300 g (10½ oz) tomatoes, chopped roughly
1 litre (1¾ pints) beef stock
75 g (2¾ oz) small dried pasta shapes
150 g (5½ oz) cooked roast beef,
    sliced thinly and cut into strips
50 g (1¾ oz) spinach, rinsed
2 tablespoons hot horseradish sauce
150 g pot 0% fat Greek yogurt

1 Spray a large lidded pan with the cooking spray and heat until hot. Add the celery, onion and pepper and stir fry for 5 minutes, adding a little water if it begins to stick. Add the garlic and tomatoes and cook for a couple more minutes until the tomatoes begin to soften.

2 Add the stock, bring to the boil then stir in the pasta. Cover and cook for 10–15 minutes until the pasta is just cooked. Stir in the beef and spinach and leave on the heat for another minute to warm through.

3 Mix the horseradish and yogurt together and serve the soup with 1 tablespoon on top.

Try this If you're not keen on horseradish, use 2 tablespoons of wholegrain mustard instead.

French onion soup with toasts

Calories per serving 247	**Serves 4**
20 mins prep, 40 mins cooking	
soup only	

low fat cooking spray

900 g (2 lb) onions, sliced

4 garlic cloves, chopped

2 fresh rosemary sprigs

2 tablespoons brandy

1.2 litres (2 pints) hot chicken stock

2 × 85 g (3¼ oz) bagels

30 g (1¼ oz) Gruyère cheese, grated

½ teaspoon English mustard powder

salt and freshly ground black pepper

You will need a piece of non stick baking parchment, cut to the same size as the pan

1 Spray a large lidded saucepan with the cooking spray and heat until hot. Add the onions and stir fry over a high heat for 3 minutes before reducing the heat to low. Stir in the garlic and rosemary.

2 Sit the baking parchment circle on top of the onions to help keep the moisture in. Cover with the lid and leave to cook for 15 minutes. Lift the paper, and give the onions a stir, cover again with the paper and lid and continue cooking for a further 15 minutes after which they should be a caramelised golden brown and super soft. If they aren't, repeat the stir, cover and cook, checking every 10 minutes.

3 Once the onions are cooked, discard the paper, increase the heat and add the brandy. Let it sizzle for a minute. Add the stock. Cover again. Cook over a low heat for 10 minutes.

4 Meanwhile, preheat the grill to medium. Slice the bagels in half horizontally and then cut each half into two pieces, for a total of eight crescents. Grill the brown, uncut side of the bagel until crispy, about a minute. Mix together the cheese and mustard and spread over the cut side of the toasts. Return to the grill to melt the cheese.

5 Season the soup. Serve in warm bowls with the toasts.

Miso bean soup

Calories per serving 183	**Serves 1**
Takes 10 mins	

Miso paste is made from soya and makes a light but warming soup. It is available in most supermarkets.

low fat cooking spray

2 spring onions, chopped

15 g sachet instant miso soup paste

200 ml (7 fl oz) boiling water

75 g (2¾ oz) silken tofu, cubed

50 g (1¾ oz) frozen soya beans

2 fresh mint leaves, shredded

1 Spray a small pan with the cooking spray and heat until hot. Add the spring onions and cook for 1 minute. Add the miso paste with the boiling water. Stir to mix.

2 Add the tofu and beans and warm through over a medium heat for about 2 minutes until the beans are hot. Stir in the mint and serve.

Herby gazpacho

Calories per serving 145	Serves 4
Takes 20 mins + 30 mins chilling	

This delightfully refreshing soup can be whizzed up quickly so it's ideal for hot days when you want an easy option.

60 g (2 oz) day old white bread
700g (1 lb 9 oz) ripe tomatoes, chopped roughly
3 spring onions, chopped
1 small garlic clove, chopped
1 yellow or orange pepper,
    de-seeded and chopped
a large handful of fresh flat leaf parsley
1 tablespoon fresh thyme leaves
600 ml (20 fl oz) tomato juice
1 teaspoon sugar
2 teaspoons sherry vinegar or white wine vinegar
10 cm (4 inch) cucumber, diced
2 teaspoons extra virgin olive oil, for drizzling
salt and freshly ground black pepper

1 Break the bread into pieces, put into a bowl and just cover in cold water. Leave to soak for 10 minutes, drain and squeeze out any excess water.

2 Place the bread in a liquidiser, or use a hand held blender, with the tomatoes, spring onions, garlic and pepper and blend to a paste. Add the parsley and thyme and blend again. Then add the tomato juice, sugar and vinegar and blend again until well combined. The texture should be smooth but with plenty of bits.

3 Season to taste, then chill for at least 30 minutes. Serve in bowls with the cucumber and a drizzle of olive oil.

Sweetcorn and smoked ham chowder

Calories per serving 177	Serves 4
10 mins prep, 25 mins cooking	

This warming soup is great comfort food.

250 g (9 oz) sweetcorn, preferably from the cob
    (see Cook's tip)
600 ml (20 fl oz) skimmed milk
600 ml (20 fl oz) vegetable stock
200 g (7 oz) potatoes, peeled and diced
1 bay leaf
110 g (4 oz) lean smoked ham, cut into small chunks
a handful of chopped fresh parsley, to garnish

1 Place the sweetcorn, milk, stock, potatoes and bay leaf in a large saucepan. Bring to the boil, reduce the heat and simmer gently for 15–20 minutes until the potatoes are cooked. Remove from the heat.

2 Discard the bay leaf, then roughly mash the soup to disperse the potato and thicken it slightly; the majority of the sweetcorn should remain whole. Return the pan to the heat, add the ham and simmer very gently for 5 minutes. Serve in large warm bowls, sprinkled with the parsley.

cook's tip...

When in season, corn on the cob is very economical to use. Simply remove the outer leaves and hair and carefully slice down the cob to remove the corn kernels. Alternatively, canned or frozen corn works well. Don't worry about defrosting frozen corn, just allow the soup to come to the boil in step 1.

Tom yam soup

Calories per serving 142

Takes 20 mins

Serves 2

You'll love this deliciously spicy and sour soup from Thailand.

low fat cooking spray
250 g (9 oz) baby button mushrooms,
    halved if large
2 spring onions, sliced
600 ml (20 fl oz) chicken or vegetable stock
1 tablespoon fish sauce
2 fresh kaffir lime leaves or 1 dried
1 lemongrass stick
2.5 cm (1 inch) fresh ginger, sliced
1 small red chilli, de-seeded and cut in rings
75 g (2¾ oz) dried Thai rice noodles, broken in half
150 g (5½ oz) cooked and peeled prawns
juice of a lime

1 Spray a non stick frying pan with the cooking spray and heat until hot. Add the mushrooms and spring onions and cook for 5 minutes until softened. Remove from the heat.

2 Place the stock, fish sauce, lime leaves, lemon grass and ginger in a large lidded pan. Bring to the boil, cover and simmer for 5 minutes.

3 Add the chilli, noodles and prawns to the mushrooms and onions. Cook gently for 2–3 minutes until hot. Remove the aromatics (lime leaves, lemon grass and ginger) before serving. Squeeze in the lime and serve in large bowls.

Try this Add 150 g (5½ oz) cooked skinless, boneless chicken breast instead of the prawns.

This soup is quick to make and the flavour is fantastic.

Leek and potato soup

Calories per serving 187   **Serves 2**
10 mins prep, 20 mins cooking
❄ soup only

Make this soup in the winter when leeks are in season – it's a great frugal recipe.

low fat cooking spray
250 g (9 oz) leeks, chopped
225 g (8 oz) potatoes, peeled or unpeeled, and diced
1 garlic clove, chopped roughly
600 ml (20 fl oz) vegetable stock
4 Parma ham slices
salt and freshly ground black pepper

1 Spray a large lidded saucepan with the cooking spray and heat until hot. Add the leeks and potatoes and cook, stirring occasionally, for 3 minutes. Add the garlic and cook for another minute before adding the stock. Bring to the boil, cover and simmer for 15 minutes until soft. Preheat the grill to medium.

2 Remove the pan from the heat and use a hand held blender, or transfer the soup to a liquidiser, and blend until smooth. Return to the heat, season and warm through.

3 Meanwhile, cook the Parma ham under the grill for about 1 minute, turning once, until crispy.

4 Serve the soup in warm bowls with the Parma ham on top.

V Try this For a vegetarian version, omit the Parma ham and serve with 15 g (½ oz) grated cheese shared between the two servings.

Hearty chicken soup

Calories per serving 191   **Serves 4**
5 mins prep, 15 mins cooking

Homemade chicken soup is always popular and very simple to make. Serve with 25 g (1 oz) finely grated Parmesan cheese, shared between the bowls.

1 litre (1¾ pints) chicken stock
2 carrots, peeled and diced
80 g (3 oz) small dried pasta shapes
300 g (10½ oz) skinless, boneless chicken
    breast, cut into strips
2 bay leaves
150 g (5½ oz) green beans, trimmed and chopped
freshly ground black pepper

1 In a large pan, bring the stock to the boil. Add the remaining ingredients, except the beans, and simmer for 10 minutes.

2 Stir in the beans and leave to cook for another 5 minutes before ladling into warmed bowls. Grind over some black pepper and serve immediately.

Lamb and barley broth

Calories per serving 157	Serves 4

10 mins prep, 50 mins cooking

You can add different vegetables to this soup. Use vegetables that are in season or simply what you have in the fridge.

low fat cooking spray
250 g (9 oz) lean lamb leg, cut into strips
1 large onion, chopped
1 carrot, peeled and chopped
2 garlic cloves, chopped
60 g (2 oz) pearl barley, rinsed in cold water
1.2 litres (2 pints) hot lamb or vegetable stock
bouquet garni (see Cook's tip)
75 g (2¾ oz) cabbage, shredded

1 Spray a large lidded pan with the cooking spray and heat until hot. Add the lamb and stir fry until brown. Add the onion and cook for 2 minutes before adding the carrot, garlic and barley. Cook for a minute then stir in the stock and the bouquet garni. Bring to the boil, cover and reduce the heat to low. Cook for 45 minutes until all is tender.
2 Remove the lid, add the cabbage and cook for 2–3 minutes until it is just tender. Discard the bouquet garni and serve the soup in large shallow bowls.

cook's tip...

You can buy bouquet garni sachets in the spice section of the supermarket or make them by tying together some fresh herbs, perhaps a bay leaf, a large rosemary sprig and some thyme sprigs.

Spiced carrot and butternut soup

Calories per serving 129	Serves 4

10 mins prep, 35 mins cooking

If you like spice, just use a hotter curry powder. Also, if you freeze spicy food it tends to get hotter, so once defrosted, it tastes spicier.

low fat cooking spray
300 g (10½ oz) carrots, peeled and chopped
400 g (14 oz) butternut squash, peeled, de-seeded and chopped
1 tablespoon medium curry powder
1.2 litres (2 pints) hot vegetable stock
2 teaspoons olive oil
2 large red onions, sliced thinly
1 teaspoon black onion seeds
½ teaspoon cumin seeds

1 Spray a large lidded saucepan with the cooking spray and heat until hot. Add the carrots, squash and curry powder and stir fry for 3 minutes. Add the stock, bring to the boil, cover and reduce the heat to simmer for 20 minutes until the vegetables are soft.
2 Transfer to a liquidiser, or use a hand held blender, and blend until smooth.
3 Heat the oil in a non stick frying pan and cook the onions over a medium high heat for 5–10 minutes until golden and crispy. Stir in the onion seeds and cumin seeds and cook for a minute.
4 Serve the soup topped with the onion mixture.

Saffron seafood bisque

Calories per serving 166
10 mins prep, 20 mins cooking

Serves 4

For a special occasion, serve this lovely soup in a large tureen. Ideal with a 40 g (1½ oz) piece of baguette per person on the side.

a pinch of saffron
low fat cooking spray
1 onion, chopped
75 ml (3 fl oz) dry sherry
400 g can chopped tomatoes
400 ml (14 fl oz) fish stock
1 fresh rosemary sprig
250 g punnet mixed seafood
200 g (7 oz) skinless, boneless white fish
**   (e.g. coley), chopped**
1 tablespoon reduced fat double cream

1 Soak the saffron in 3 tablespoons of warm water for 5 minutes.

2 Spray a large lidded pan with the cooking spray and heat until hot. Add the onion and stir fry for 10 minutes until beginning to soften, adding a little water if it starts to stick. Add the sherry, letting it bubble up, then add the tomatoes, fish stock and rosemary along with the saffron and its soaking water. Cover and simmer gently for 10 minutes.

3 Stir in the seafood and fish and simmer gently for 5 minutes until the fish is just cooked. Remove from the heat and stir in the cream. Serve in large bowls.

cooking
for me

Turn to these recipes for some great ideas when you're cooking for yourself. They're all incredibly tasty and quick to cook. The fabulously fresh-tasting Griddled Steak and Peach Salad can be on the table in just 10 minutes and the Pot Roasted Vegetables with Lamb Steaks is even easier – simply spend 10 minutes prepping then let it cook by itself while you put up your feet.

Courgette and pea risotto on page 68

Halloumi skewers with mango dressing

Calories per serving 461
20 mins prep, 15 mins cooking
 Serves 1

110 g (4 oz) baby new potatoes
2 teaspoons reduced fat mayonnaise
1 teaspoon curry powder
75 g (2¾ oz) halloumi light, cubed
6 cherry tomatoes
2 spring onions, cut into 2 cm (¾ inch) lengths

For the dressing

100 g (3½ oz) mango, peeled, stoned and chopped
2 teaspoons white wine vinegar
1 tablespoon mango chutney
finely grated zest of half a lime

To serve

1 Little Gem lettuce, divided into leaves
8 cucumber slices

You will need two small skewers (soak wooden ones in cold water for 20 minutes first)

1 Bring a lidded pan of water to the boil. Add the potatoes, bring back to the boil, cover and simmer for 10–15 minutes until just cooked. Drain well.

2 Mix together the mayonnaise and curry powder in a large bowl and stir in the potatoes to coat. Preheat the grill to medium.

3 Thread the halloumi, tomatoes and spring onions on to the skewers.

4 Place the ingredients for the dressing in a small blender, or use a hand held blender, to blend until smooth. Brush over the skewers and grill for 4–5 minutes, turning frequently, until lightly charred.

5 Serve the skewers with the warm potatoes, the lettuce and cucumber. Drizzle over any remaining dressing.

Sweet and sour duck with pineapple

Calories per serving 465
Takes 15 mins
Serves 1

It's best to prepare all the ingredients before you start.

50 g (1¾ oz) dried egg noodles
low fat cooking spray
125 g (4½ oz) skinless, boneless duck
    breast, cut into thin slices
1 small carrot, peeled and cut into thin strips
½ yellow pepper, de-seeded and chopped thinly
1 tablespoon white wine or rice vinegar
2 teaspoons brown sugar
2 teaspoons tomato ketchup
1 teaspoon soy sauce
1 pineapple ring from a can in natural juice,
    chopped
1 spring onion, sliced finely

1 Bring a pan of water to the boil, add the noodles and cook according to the packet instructions. Drain and cover to keep warm.

2 Meanwhile, spray a small wok or non stick frying pan with the cooking spray and heat until hot. Add the duck and stir fry for 2 minutes over a high heat. Add the carrot and pepper and cook for another 3 minutes until softened.

3 In a jug, mix together the vinegar, sugar, ketchup and soy sauce and then add to the pan with the pineapple pieces. Cook for a minute or two until sizzling hot. Remove from the heat and serve with the noodles, sprinkling over the spring onion.

V Try this For a vegetarian version, make this recipe with two 100 g (3½ oz) Quorn fillets, cut into pieces, instead of the duck.

Pot roasted vegetables with lamb steaks

Calories per serving 460	Serves 1
10 mins prep, 1 hr cooking	

Try this Pot roasting is a great way to cook meat and vegetables. Use this recipe to cook a 150 g (5½ oz) skinless, boneless chicken breast instead of the lamb.

Even if you are only cooking for yourself, you might just fancy a roast and this recipe makes it easy.

1 small carrot, peeled and chopped into chunks
75 g (2¾ oz) parsnip, peeled and sliced
1 celery stick, chopped into chunks
1 small leek, trimmed and chopped
100 g (3½ oz) sweet potato, peeled
   and chopped into chunks
low fat cooking spray
1 tablespoon wholegrain mustard
150 ml (5 fl oz) vegetable stock
75 g (2¾ oz) butternut squash, peeled,
   de-seeded and chopped
150 g (5½ oz) lamb leg steak, visible fat removed
salt and freshly ground black pepper
2 teaspoons redcurrant jelly, to serve

1 Preheat the oven to Gas Mark 6/200°C/fan oven 180°C. Place all the vegetables except the butternut squash in a roasting tin so that they sit snugly in one layer. Spray with the cooking spray and roast for 30 minutes, stirring half way through.

2 Mix together the mustard and stock. Remove the tin from the oven and pour the mixture over the vegetables, adding the butternut squash. Top with the lamb steak, season and roast for 20–30 minutes until the lamb is cooked and the vegetables are tender. Serve with the redcurrant jelly on the side.

This satisfying meal is a pleasure to make for yourself.

Minted chicken and bean salad

Calories per serving 298   Serves 1
Takes 20 mins

Serve this warm or mix together, cool and chill before packing into a lunchbox, keeping the leaves separate.

150 ml (5 fl oz) chicken stock
150 g (5½ oz) skinless, boneless chicken
    breast, cut into four
40 g (1½ oz) green beans, trimmed and halved
1 head Little Gem lettuce, leaves separated
3 cherry tomatoes, halved
1 fresh parsley sprig, chopped
1 fresh mint sprig, chopped
2 teaspoons reduced fat mayonnaise
1 teaspoon wholegrain mustard

1   Bring the stock to the boil in a small lidded pan. Add the chicken, cover and simmer gently for 7 minutes. Add the beans, bring back to the boil and cook for a further 3 minutes until the chicken is cooked through and the beans are tender.
2   Drain, discarding the stock. Once cool enough to handle, pull the chicken into strips. Arrange the lettuce and tomatoes on a serving plate.
3   Mix together the herbs, mayonnaise and mustard and stir in the chicken and beans. Serve on top of the leaves.

Try this Make this salad with 40 g (1½ oz) fresh or frozen broad beans instead of green beans.

Cheesy pesto mushrooms

Calories per serving 291   Serves 1
Takes 15 mins

Fresh, quick and easy. Serve the pesto mushrooms with 40 g (1½ oz) dried pasta, cooked and tossed with 2 teaspoons of snipped chives.

low fat cooking spray
110 g (4 oz) large field mushrooms,
    stalks removed
25 g (1 oz) soft goat's cheese
15 g (½ oz) fresh wholemeal breadcrumbs

For the pesto
15 g (½ oz) pine nut kernels
15 g (½ oz) chopped fresh flat leaf parsley
15 g (½ oz) Parmesan cheese, chopped roughly
1 small garlic clove, crushed

1   To make the pesto, dry fry the pine nuts for 2–3 minutes in a non stick frying pan, stirring regularly, until golden.
2   Place the parsley, pine nut kernels, Parmesan cheese and garlic in a small food processor or liquidiser, or use a hand held blender. Blend to a rough paste.
3   Preheat the grill to medium and line the grill pan with foil. Spray the topside of the mushrooms with the cooking spray, then grill for about 2 minutes until beginning to soften. Turn them over, spray the underside and cook for a minute or so until juicy.
4   Top the mushrooms with the pesto and crumble over the goat's cheese. Sprinkle the breadcrumbs on top and grill for another 1–2 minutes until bubbling. Serve warm.

Pesto turkey fillet

Calories per serving 440   Serves 1
Takes 25 mins

A good handful of spinach leaves are ideal to serve on the side.

50 g (1¾ oz) trofie or penne pasta
50 g (1¾ oz) green beans, chopped
low fat cooking spray
125 g (4½ oz) turkey fillet, cut into thin strips
4 cherry tomatoes, halved

For the pesto
10 g (¼ oz) pine nut kernels
10 g (¼ oz) Parmesan cheese
15 g (½ oz) fresh basil, chopped roughly,
    with a couple of leaves reserved for garnish

1 To make the pesto, in a non stick frying pan, dry fry the pine nut kernels for 2–3 minutes over a low heat, stirring regularly until golden. Set aside.

2 Place the pine nut kernels and Parmesan in a small food processor, or use a hand held blender, and whizz until chopped. Add the basil, pushing it down, and whizz again. Add 2 teaspoons of water and blend to a rough paste. Set aside.

3 Bring a pan of water to the boil, add the pasta and cook according to the packet instructions, adding the beans for the final 3 minutes of cooking time. Drain well.

4 Meanwhile, spray a small non stick frying pan with the cooking spray and heat until hot. Add the turkey strips and stir fry for 3 minutes until just cooked through.

5 Add the cherry tomatoes and cook for another minute to soften. Stir in the pesto with the pasta and warm through over a low heat for a minute or so. Serve immediately with basil to garnish.

Prawn teriyaki

Calories per serving 279   Serves 1
Takes 20 mins

Teriyaki sauce is a great store cupboard stand by. Use it in stir fries or simply add it to plain noodles or rice.

40 g (1½ oz) dried long grain rice
low fat cooking spray
150 g (5½ oz) mixed stir fry vegetables
    e.g. peppers, beansprouts, greens
110 g (4 oz) raw tiger prawns, defrosted if frozen
2 tablespoons teriyaki sauce

1 Bring a pan of water to the boil, add the rice and cook for 10–12 minutes or according to the packet instructions. Drain well and keep warm.

2 Meanwhile, spray a wok or non stick frying pan with the cooking spray and heat until hot. Add the vegetables and stir fry over a high heat for a minute then add the prawns and cook them for 2–3 minutes until they have turned pink.

3 Add the teriyaki sauce and heat through. Serve the rice with the teriyaki mixture on top.

cook's tip...

Buy the quantity of prawns you need at the fish counter or keep a bag in the freezer. To defrost, simply soak in very hot water for a few minutes.

Courgette and pea risotto

Calories per serving 424   Serves 1
Takes 40 mins

A satisfying and flavoursome dish. You can omit the vermouth, if you prefer.

low fat cooking spray
1 small courgette, trimmed and diced
1 garlic clove, crushed
½ teaspoon dried thyme
75 g (2¾ oz) dried risotto rice
30 ml (1 fl oz) vermouth or dry white wine (optional)
250 ml (9 fl oz) hot vegetable stock
1 tablespoon fresh thyme leaves or
    1 teaspoon dried thyme
40 g (1½ oz) frozen peas, defrosted
15 g (½ oz) pecorino cheese, cut into shavings
salt and freshly ground black pepper

1 Spray a large non stick frying pan with the cooking spray and heat until hot. Add the courgettes and fry for 3–4 minutes. Add the garlic and thyme and cook for a further minute until golden, then remove from the pan and set aside.

2 Spray the pan again with the cooking spray. Add the rice. Stir to coat in any remaining juices then add the vermouth or wine, if using. Let it sizzle for a minute before adding a ladleful of stock. Simmer for 2–3 minutes, stirring occasionally until nearly all the stock has been absorbed.

3 Add another ladleful and continue cooking as before. If the rice is still not cooked to your liking when you have only one ladleful of stock left, add a little hot water. With the final ladleful of stock, stir in the fresh thyme, the peas and the courgette mixture. When ready, the rice should still have some bite but not be 'crunchy' or 'hard' in the middle.

4 Season the risotto and serve with the cheese on top.

Orzo and celeriac slaw

Calories per serving 373   Serves 1
Takes 15 mins

Orzo means 'barley' in Italian. It is delicious in soups and stews as well as salads. Serve with a grilled 165 g (5¾ oz) skinless, boneless chicken breast.

60 g (2 oz) dried orzo pasta
50 g (1¾ oz) celeriac, cut into thin strips
1 carrot, peeled and cut into thin strips
50 g (1¾ oz) green or white cabbage, shredded finely
2 teaspoons reduced fat mayonnaise
2 teaspoons 0% fat Greek yogurt
1 teaspoon wholegrain or Dijon mustard
a handful of rocket leaves
a squeeze of lemon juice
freshly ground black pepper

1 Bring a pan of water to the boil, add the orzo and cook according to the packet instructions. Drain and rinse in cold water until the pasta is cold.

2 Mix the vegetables in a bowl. Stir in the mayonnaise, yogurt, mustard, some black pepper and the orzo and mix well. Serve with the rocket leaves and the lemon juice squeezed over.

cook's tip...

This makes a great lunchbox and could be made the night before – remember to pack the rocket leaves separately though, otherwise they will wilt.

Griddled steak and peach salad

Calories per serving 230	**Serves 1**
Takes 10 mins	

Griddling is fast and uses very little fat. Serve with two rye crispbreads.

25 g (1 oz) rocket leaves
10 cm (4 inch) cucumber, cut into batons
4 cherry tomatoes, halved
2 teaspoons hot horseradish
1 tablespoon 0% fat Greek yogurt
2 fresh mint leaves, shredded
low fat cooking spray
110 g (4 oz) minute steak, visible fat removed
1 peach (about 150 g/5½ oz), stoned
   and cut into wedges

1 Arrange the rocket, cucumber and tomatoes on a serving plate. In a bowl, mix together the horseradish, yogurt and mint.
2 Heat a griddle pan or non stick frying pan until hot. Spray the steak on both sides with the cooking spray. Cook in the pan for a minute, turning once until browned but still juicy. Remove from the pan, cover and rest for 2 minutes.
3 Spray the peach wedges with the cooking spray and add to the same pan. Cook for 30 seconds to 1 minute before turning, cooking just long enough to mark or brown them. Remove from the pan and arrange on top of the salad.
4 Slice the steak into strips and serve on top of the salad with the horseradish dressing spooned over.

Try this If you don't like the heat of horseradish, use 1 tablespoon of wholegrain mustard in the yogurt instead.

Smoked haddock pilaff

Calories per serving 335 Serves 1
Takes 30 mins

An easy and tasty one pan dish.

low fat cooking spray
½ red onion, sliced
2 whole cardamom pods, crushed lightly
½ teaspoon cumin seeds
1 teaspoon garam masala
40 g (1½ oz) dried basmati rice
250 ml (9 fl oz) vegetable stock
60 g (2 oz) green beans, trimmed and chopped
100 g (3½ oz) skinless smoked haddock fillet,
    cut into chunks
25 g (1 oz) frozen sweetcorn, defrosted
1 tablespoon chopped fresh parsley

1 Spray a medium sized, non stick lidded saucepan with the cooking spray and heat until hot. Add the onion and cook for 5 minutes until softened, adding a splash of water if it starts to stick.

2 Add the spices and cook for a minute, before adding the rice. Stir to coat then add the stock. Bring to the boil, cover and cook for 8 minutes. Add the beans and fish. Cover again. Continue cooking for 3–4 minutes until everything is cooked through. Most of the water should have been absorbed but drain any that hasn't.

3 Remove from the heat, flake the fish, stir in the sweetcorn and leave to heat through for about 2 minutes. Serve the pilaff, garnished with the parsley.

V Try this For a vegetarian option, omit the fish, adding 100 g (3½ oz) smoked tofu, cubed, with the beans.

Spiced beef larb

Calories per serving 398 Serves 1
Takes 20 mins
 meat only

Larb is from Laos and Thailand where mince is cooked with spices until deliciously crispy.

low fat cooking spray
175 g (6 oz) lean beef mince
½ beef stock cube, crumbled
1 small red chilli, de-seeded and diced
1½ teaspoons diced fresh ginger
1 garlic clove, diced
1 tablespoon hoisin sauce
a handful of fresh coriander leaves
4 or 5 small lettuce leaves, e.g. Little Gem
1 carrot, peeled and cut into thin sticks
2 spring onions, sliced
4 fresh mint leaves, shredded

1 Spray a non stick frying pan with the cooking spray and heat until hot. Add the beef and stir fry over a high heat for 5 minutes until browned and cooked through. Add the stock cube with 2 tablespoons of water, chilli, ginger and garlic and cook for another minute. Remove from the heat and stir in the hoisin sauce and half the coriander leaves.

2 Arrange the lettuce leaves and carrot sticks on a plate, top with the mince and garnish with the spring onions, mint and remaining coriander. Serve immediately.

Hot prawn pots

Calories per serving 247   **Serves 1**
Takes 15 mins

If you fancy a cheesy topping, sprinkle over 10 g (¼ oz) finely grated Parmesan cheese. Little Gem leaves, grated carrot and cucumber, drizzled with a little lemon juice, make a nice salad on the side.

low fat cooking spray
15 g (½ oz) low fat spread
15 g (½ oz) plain flour
150 ml (5 fl oz) skimmed milk
finely grated zest of ½ a lemon
1 tablespoon chopped fresh parsley
60 g (2 oz) cooked, peeled prawns, defrosted if frozen
25 g (1 oz) sweetcorn, defrosted if frozen
15 g (½ oz) bread, diced
salt and freshly ground black pepper

You will need a ramekin with a 10 cm (4 inch) diameter

1. Spray the ramekin with the cooking spray and set aside.
2. Melt the low fat spread in a small pan. Add the flour and blend with the spread. Cook, stirring for a minute before removing from the heat. Gradually add the milk, a little at a time, blending to a smooth paste before adding more. Once all the milk has been added, return to the heat and bring gently to boil, stirring continuously until thickened.
3. Add the lemon zest, parsley, prawns and sweetcorn and warm through until hot.
4. Preheat the grill to medium. Spoon the prawn mixture into the ramekin, top with the bread then spray with the cooking spray and grill for a minute or so until golden. Serve immediately.

family food

As life gets busier, making time to sit down and enjoy meals with loved ones is increasingly important. The recipes in this chapter are ideal for those times and there's something here for everyone. The Pork Lasagne or Meatball Pasta Bake are great choices and they're sure to become family favourites. Vegetarians will happily tuck into some Potato and Pea Curry or they can enjoy the irresistible Cheese and Onion Strudel. With choices like these, cooking for you and your family isn't only fun, it's rewarding.

Pork lasagne

Calories per serving 320   **Serves 4**
20 mins prep, 50 mins cooking
❄

Serve with a salad made with romaine lettuce, red onion, cut into rings, and tomatoes on the vine, quartered.

350 g (12 oz) lean pork mince
1 large onion, chopped
2 carrots, peeled and grated
80 g (3 oz) swede, peeled and grated
2 garlic cloves, crushed
700 g jar passata with herbs
75 g (2¾ oz) no pre-cook lasagne sheets
100 ml (3½ fl oz) half fat crème fraîche
25 g (1 oz) Parmesan cheese, grated finely

You will need a 2.5 litre (4½ pint) deep square or rectangular ovenproof dish

1 Heat a large non stick frying pan until hot. Add the pork mince and stir fry over a high heat for 5 minutes, breaking up any lumps, until browned all over. Add the onion and cook for another 3 minutes.

2 Stir in the carrots, swede and garlic and continue cooking over a lower heat for about 5 minutes until all the vegetables have softened. Stir in 500 g (1 lb 2 oz) of the passata, bring to the boil and remove from the heat.

3 Preheat the oven to Gas Mark 6/200°C/fan oven 180°C. Spoon a third of the meat mixture into the ovenproof dish, top with a layer of lasagne and repeat twice more, ending with the final lasagne sheets. Pour over the remaining passata.

4 Mix the crème fraîche with 2 tablespoons of warm water and spread over the top. Scatter over the cheese and bake for 45–50 minutes until golden and bubbling. Serve immediately.

cook's tip...

❄ **To freeze, cool completely. Place the whole dish in a freezer bag and store it for up to a month. Defrost thoroughly, cover with foil and warm through in the oven.**

Pork gives this lasagne a delicious sweetness.
The whole family will love it.

Slow roast lamb

Calories per serving 447   Serves 4
20 mins prep, 2 hrs 20 mins cooking
 meat only

Slow roasting meat on the bone makes it deliciously tender. Serve it with a portion of steamed broccoli each.

850 g (1 lb 12½ oz) half lamb leg, visible fat removed
15 g (½ oz) anchovies in brine, cut into pieces
2 fresh rosemary sprigs
300 g (10½ oz) sweet potatoes, peeled and cut into chunks
250 g (9 oz) parsnips, peeled and cut into chunks
2 red peppers, de-seeded and chopped
2 onions, quartered
1 garlic bulb, sliced horizontally
low fat cooking spray
4 teaspoons gravy granules
freshly ground black pepper

You will need two roasting tins; a roasting rack

1 Preheat the oven to Gas Mark 7/220°C/fan oven 200°C. Place the lamb on a rack over a roasting tin.
2 Make deep incisions in the lamb and push in pieces of the anchovy and small sprigs from half of the rosemary. Season all over with black pepper. Cook for 20 minutes until beginning to brown, then reduce the oven to Gas Mark 3/160°C/fan oven 140°C and roast for 1 hour.
3 Place the vegetables and garlic in a large roasting tray with the remaining rosemary. Spray with the cooking spray. Roast in the oven below the meat for another hour.
4 Make up the gravy according to the packet instructions. Serve 125 g (4½ oz) of the meat per person with the vegetables and gravy poured over.

Pork with sweet potato mash

Calories per serving 499   Serves 4
15 mins prep, 35 mins cooking

Delicious with steamed broccoli and baby carrots.

low fat cooking spray
2 red onions, cut into thin wedges
2 eating apples (125 g/4½ oz each), cored and cut into wedges
4 × 125 g (4½ oz) pork loin chops, visible fat removed
a fresh rosemary sprig
a fresh thyme sprig
1 tablespoon chopped fresh flat leaf parsley
8 fresh sage leaves, chopped
25 g (1 oz) low fat spread
750 g (1 lb 10 oz) sweet potato, peeled and chopped
salt and freshly ground black pepper

1 Preheat the oven to Gas Mark 6/200°C/fan oven 180°C. Spray a non stick frying pan with the cooking spray and heat until hot. Add the onion and cook, stirring occasionally, for 5 minutes until softened and beginning to brown. Add a little water if they begin to stick. Remove from the heat and spoon into an ovenproof dish that will hold the pork chops in one layer.
2 Mix the apples into the onions and season with some black pepper. Top with the pork chops. Mix together all the herbs and the low fat spread to a paste and spread it over the chops. Bake in the oven for 25–30 minutes until the chops are cooked through.
3 Meanwhile, bring a lidded pan of water to the boil and add the sweet potatoes. Cover and simmer until just soft, about 10–15 minutes. Drain well, mash and season.
4 Serve the chops with the onions and apples and the mash on the side. Spoon over any juices.

Cheese and onion strudel

Calories per serving 324	**Serves 4**
25 mins prep, 30 mins cooking	

Enjoy with a quick coleslaw made with shredded cabbage, carrots and a little sliced onion, mixed with 2 tablespoons of 0% fat Greek yogurt per person.

750 g (1 lb 10 oz) floury potatoes
   (Désirée or King Edwards), peeled and diced
low fat cooking spray
2 red onions, chopped
1 garlic clove, crushed
1 tablespoon fresh thyme leaves
   or 1 teaspoon dried thyme
1 green chilli, de-seeded and diced
3 × 45 g (1½ oz) sheets filo pastry, measuring
   50 × 24 cm (20 × 9½ inch), defrosted if frozen
60 g (2 oz) half fat mature Cheddar cheese, grated

1 Bring a large lidded pan of water to the boil and add the potatoes. Bring back to the boil, cover and simmer for 5 minutes until just cooked. Drain well and pat dry with kitchen paper.

2 Spray a large non stick frying pan with the cooking spray and heat until hot. Add the onions and stir fry for 5 minutes, adding a little water if it begins to stick. Add the garlic, thyme and chilli. Cook for another 2 minutes. Add the potatoes and fry for 2–3 minutes until they begin to brown. Set aside to cool slightly.

3 Preheat the oven to Gas Mark 6/200°C/fan oven 180°C. Spray a baking sheet with the cooking spray. Lay a sheet of filo on the tray, spray with the cooking spray and top with another sheet. Repeat to give three layers. Take half of the potato mixture, form it into a log shape and then spoon down the middle of the pastry.

4 Top with the cheese and then add the remaining potato. Bring the sides of the pastry up and over to create a log, tucking the ends under to secure them. Spray with the cooking spray and bake for 20–30 minutes until golden. Serve in slices.

Floury potatoes such as Désirée or King Edward work best in this recipe. When diced, they retain some shape but also soften well in the frying pan, creating lots of crispy bits.

Cheesy potato and courgette gratin

Calories per serving 212	Serves 4
15 mins prep, 1 hr 10 mins cooking	

This supper dish can be made in advance and then simply reheated. Serve each with a grilled 165 g (5¾ oz) skinless, boneless chicken breast.

low fat cooking spray
2 courgettes, sliced thinly
300 ml (10 fl oz) skimmed milk
1 vegetable stock cube, crumbled
700 g (1 lb 9 oz) floury potatoes, peeled and sliced
3 garlic cloves, sliced
60 g (2 oz) soft goat's cheese, crumbled
salt and freshly ground black pepper

You will need a 2 litre (3½ pint) ceramic ovenproof dish

1 Preheat the oven to Gas Mark 5/190°C/fan oven 170°C. Spray the ovenproof dish with the cooking spray and place on a baking sheet.

2 Spray a large non stick frying pan with the cooking spray and heat until hot. Add the courgettes and cook over a medium heat, turning occasionally until browned.

3 Warm the milk in a pan. Stir in the crumbled stock cube.

4 Layer the potatoes, courgettes and garlic in the ovenproof dish, seasoning the layers as you go. Pour over the milk, cover with foil and cook for 50 minutes or until just tender. Scatter over the cheese and bake uncovered for about 20 minutes or until golden, making sure that it doesn't get too dry. Serve immediately.

Ⓥ Try this This recipe also works well using 350 g (12 oz) sweet potato and 350 g (12 oz) potatoes, instead of the floury potatoes.

Meatball pasta bake

Calories per serving 454	Serves 4
20 mins prep, 30 mins cooking	

Enjoy with a crunchy salad of thin carrot sticks, strips of cucumber and red or yellow pepper on the side.

400 g (14 oz) lean beef mince
1 large onion, chopped finely
1 tablespoon chopped fresh parsley
½ teaspoon dried oregano
low fat cooking spray
175 g (6 oz) dried penne pasta
2 × 400 g cans chopped tomatoes
2 garlic cloves, chopped
125 g pack mozzarella light, drained and chopped
salt and freshly ground black pepper

You will need a 1.5 litre (2¾ pint) ovenproof dish

1 In a large bowl, mix together the beef, onion and herbs with some seasoning. Shape into 16 walnut sized balls.

2 Spray a non stick frying pan with the cooking spray and heat until hot. Add the meatballs and cook for 7–8 minutes until browned all over; don't worry if they are not cooked through as they will continue cooking in the oven. Remove from the heat and set aside.

3 Preheat the oven to Gas Mark 5/190°C/fan oven 170°C. Bring a pan of water to the boil, add the pasta and cook for 5 minutes or about half the cooking time stated on the packet. Drain well and mix with the tomatoes and garlic.

4 Spoon the pasta mixture into the ovenproof dish. Nestle the meatballs into the pasta, top with the mozzarella and bake for 25–30 minutes until bubbling.

Try this Use the same quantity of chicken mince for the meatballs instead of the beef.

Curried rice and chicken

Calories per serving 327   Serves 4
10 mins prep, 1 hr 15 mins cooking
❄

With such a quick prep time, this is a fantastic family dish.

low fat cooking spray
1 large onion, sliced
2 garlic cloves, crushed
1 tablespoon medium curry powder
400 ml (14 fl oz) hot chicken stock
125 g (4½ oz) dried basmati rice
200 g (7 oz) cauliflower florets
4 × 110 g (4 oz) skinless chicken drumsticks
4 × 110 g (4 oz) skinless chicken thighs (bone in)
a handful of fresh coriander leaves, to serve

You will need a large ovenproof dish

1 Preheat the oven to Gas Mark 4/180°C/fan oven 160°C.
2 Spray a large non stick frying pan with the cooking spray and heat until hot. Add the onion and cook for about 5 minutes until softened, adding a little water if it begins to stick. Stir in the garlic and curry powder and cook for a minute. Pour in the stock, stirring to scrape up the bits.
3 Place the rice and cauliflower in the bottom of the large ovenproof dish. Pour over the stock and onions. Stir to mix.
4 Rinse and dry the frying pan and spray with the cooking spray. Heat until hot, add the chicken pieces and brown all over. Add the chicken to the dish, nestling the pieces down into the rice. Cover with foil and bake for an hour. After an hour, check the rice. If it is still slightly crunchy, cover again and cook for another 15 minutes before checking again.
5 Scatter over the coriander and serve.

Try this Enjoy with four 125 g (4½ oz) skinless, boneless chicken breasts instead of drumsticks and thighs and follow the recipe as it is.

Moroccan lamb skewers

Calories per serving 493   Serves 4
Takes 20 mins
❄ meat only

Quick and easy to make, these skewers are great under the grill or you can cook them on the barbecue.

500 g (1 lb 2 oz) lean lamb mince
1 tablespoon Moroccan spices
2 eggs, beaten
2 tablespoons chopped fresh parsley
½ a kettleful of boiling water
250 g (9 oz) dried couscous
finely grated zest and juice of 1 lemon
20 cm (8 inch) cucumber, diced
20 cherry tomatoes, halved
6 tablespoons 0% fat Greek yogurt
1 tablespoon chopped fresh mint
salt and freshly ground black pepper
1 lemon, cut into wedges, to serve

You will need four metal skewers

1 Preheat the grill to medium. Put the lamb in a bowl with the spices, eggs and parsley, then season. Mix together using your hands. Squeeze the mixture on to four metal skewers in sausage shapes. Cook the skewers under the grill for 10 minutes, turning regularly, until browned and cooked through.
2 Meanwhile, pour 100 ml (3½ fl oz) boiling water over the couscous in a bowl, stir in the lemon zest and juice and cover with cling film for 10 minutes. Fluff up the couscous using a fork and stir in the cucumber and tomatoes.
3 Mix the yogurt and mint together. Serve a skewer each on a pile of couscous with a lemon wedge to squeeze over and the yogurt dip on the side.

Try this You can make these with lean beef mince instead of lamb.

Paella with chorizo

Calories per serving 349   Serves 4
15 mins prep, 35 mins cooking

This is delicious with a fresh green salad of mixed leaves,
dressed with a drizzle of red wine vinegar.

low fat cooking spray
200 g (7 oz) skinless, boneless chicken breast,
    cut into chunks
1 onion, sliced
1 green pepper, de-seeded and sliced
1 red pepper, de-seeded and sliced
2 garlic cloves, crushed
25 g (1 oz) chorizo, diced
175 g (6 oz) dried paella or Arborio rice
400 g can chopped tomatoes with herbs
450 ml (16 fl oz) chicken stock
250 g (9 oz) mixed seafood, frozen or fresh
salt and freshly ground black pepper
2 tablespoons chopped fresh parsley, to garnish

1 Spray a large non stick frying pan with the cooking
spray and heat until hot. Add the chicken and stir fry for
5 minutes until browned. Remove from the pan and set
aside.

2 Spray the pan again with the cooking spray, add the
onion and peppers and cook for 3 minutes. Add the garlic,
chorizo and a splash of water. Cook for 2 minutes. Stir in the
rice, followed by the tomatoes, stock and chicken. Reduce
the heat to a gentle simmer and cook, stirring occasionally,
for 25–30 minutes until the rice is just tender.

3 Add the seafood and cook for 5 minutes until hot (it
may need a little longer if frozen). Add extra stock or hot
water if it gets too dry. Season and serve sprinkled with
the parsley.

Each region in Spain seems to have its own version of paella. This one uses chorizo for a lovely, smoky flavour.

Spanish chicken with peppers

> **Calories per serving 299** **Serves 4**
> 15 mins prep, 1 hr cooking
>

Serve with 40 g (1½ oz) dried brown rice per person, cooked according to the packet instructions, and steamed green beans.

2 red peppers, de-seeded and chopped
2 yellow peppers, de-seeded and chopped
1 green pepper, de-seeded and chopped
6 large tomatoes on the vine, halved
    (about 450 g/1 lb in total)
4 garlic cloves, unpeeled
2 fresh thyme sprigs
2 bay leaves
low fat cooking spray
1 tablespoon olive oil
450 g (1 lb) skinless chicken drumsticks
450 g (1 lb) skinless chicken thighs (bone in)
75 ml (3 fl oz) red wine
125 ml (4 fl oz) chicken stock
salt and freshly ground black pepper

You will need a large roasting dish

1 Preheat the oven to Gas Mark 6/200°C/fan oven 180°C. Place the peppers, tomatoes, garlic, thyme and bay leaves in the roasting dish and spray with the cooking spray. Season and roast for 20 minutes. Meanwhile, heat the oil in a large frying pan until hot. Add the chicken and brown for 4–5 minutes, turning regularly. Remove from the heat.
2 Stir the vegetables, mix in the wine and stock. Nestle the chicken, and any pan juices, into the vegetables. Cook for 30–40 minutes until the chicken is cooked through.

Try this You could also use 150 g (5½ oz) skinless, boneless chicken breasts. The timings will remain the same.

Chilli bean and beef hot pot

> **Calories per serving 310** **Serves 6**
> 20 mins prep, 1½ hrs cooking
> hot pot only

This is a proper winter warmer – just adjust the chilli according to how spicy you like it.

low fat cooking spray
600 g (1 lb 5 oz) lean braising steak, cubed
2 × 400 g cans chopped tomatoes with herbs
400 g can kidney beans, drained
3 red or mixed peppers, de-seeded and chopped
1–2 red chillies, de-seeded and diced
250 ml (9 fl oz) beef stock

For the tortilla chips
3 × 55 g (1¾ oz) pitta breads
2 teaspoons smoked or normal paprika

You will need a large, lidded, flameproof and ovenproof pan

1 Preheat the oven to Gas Mark 3/160°C/fan oven 140°C. Spray the pan with the cooking spray and heat on the hob until hot. Add the beef and cook, stirring occasionally, for 3–5 minutes until browned on all sides. You may need to do this in batches.
2 Add the tomatoes, beans, peppers, chilli and stock and bring to the boil. Remove from the heat, cover and cook in the oven for 1½ hours until the meat is really tender.
3 Meanwhile, split the pitta breads and cut each half into eight triangles. Place on a baking sheet and spray with the cooking spray. Sprinkle over the paprika and bake above the beef pan for 5–10 minutes until golden and crisp.
4 Serve the hot pot with the tortilla chips on the side.

Try this Serve with 40 g (1½ oz) dried brown rice per person, cooked according to the packet instructions, instead of tortilla chips.

Butternut squash bake

Calories per serving 255	Serves 4
15 mins prep, 1 hr cooking	

low fat cooking spray
1 carrot, peeled and diced
1 onion, chopped
1 celery stick, chopped
2 garlic cloves, chopped
1 teaspoon mixed dried herbs
350 g bag frozen Quorn mince
400 g can chopped tomatoes
1 vegetable cube, dissolved in 50 ml (2 fl oz) hot water
800 g (1 lb 11 oz) butternut squash, peeled,
    de-seeded and sliced thinly along its length
200 g (7 oz) tomatoes, sliced
30 g (1¼ oz) fresh breadcrumbs
30 g (1¼ oz) half fat Cheddar cheese, grated finely

You will need a 2 litre (3½ pint) flameproof and
ovenproof dish

1 Spray a large, lidded non stick pan with the cooking
spray and heat until hot. Add the carrot, onion and celery
and cook, stirring for 3 minutes. Add a little water and
garlic and cook for another 2 minutes. Stir in the herbs,
mince, tomatoes and stock. Bring to the boil, cover and
simmer for 20 minutes.

2 Spoon a third of the mince mixture into the ovenproof
dish. Top with a couple of slices of squash and repeat the
layers ending with the squash. Scatter over the sliced
tomatoes, the breadcrumbs and finally the cheese. Bake
for 30–40 minutes until the squash is tender and the top
is golden.

Try this Omit the Quorn and use 400 g (14 oz) lean beef
mince, adding it after the onions and celery in step 1. Fry
for 5 minutes to brown before adding the garlic.

Potato and pea curry

Calories per serving 207	Serves 4
10 mins prep, 1 hr cooking	

An easy, all-in-one curry which makes a great vegetarian
main. It's also delicious with equal amounts of potatoes
and sweet potatoes, chopped, instead of new potatoes.

1 teaspoon cumin seed
½ teaspoon chilli flakes
1 teaspoon fennel seeds
1 teaspoon black onion seed
600 g (1 lb 5 oz) new potatoes, halved if large
2 large onions, chopped
450 g (1 lb) tomatoes, chopped
500 ml (18 fl oz) vegetable stock
2 bay leaves
200 g (7 oz) frozen peas, defrosted
a handful of fresh coriander, chopped roughly

You will need a mortar and pestle or a rolling pin

1 Preheat the oven to Gas Mark 5/190°C/fan oven 170°C.
Dry fry the spices in a small non stick frying pan for a
minute or so until aromatic. Transfer to a mortar and pestle
or crush with the end of a rolling pin in a bowl and grind to
break it up; they don't need to be finely ground.
2 Place the potatoes, onions and tomatoes in a large
lidded ovenproof dish. Scatter over the seeds and toss to
mix. Pour over the stock and tuck in the bay leaves. Cover
and bake for 50 minutes until the potatoes are tender.
3 Remove the lid, stir in the peas and return to the oven,
uncovered, for 10 minutes until the peas are hot.
4 Stir in the coriander and serve.

Bobotie

Calories per serving 391   **Serves 4**
15 mins prep, 25 mins cooking

Discover a new way to enjoy beef mince in this lovely South African recipe. Serve with a portion of steamed green beans.

400 g (14 oz) lean beef mince
2 onions, chopped finely
2 garlic cloves, chopped
1 parsnip, peeled and grated
1 carrot, peeled and grated
5 cm (2 inches) fresh ginger, grated
1 teaspoon finely grated lemon zest
1 tablespoon garam masala
60 g (2 oz) sultanas
100 ml (3½ fl oz) beef stock

For the topping
250 ml pot buttermilk
2 eggs, beaten
2 teaspoons mild curry powder
15 g (½ oz) flaked almonds
salt and freshly ground black pepper

You will need a 1.5 litre (2¾ pint) deep ovenproof dish

1 Preheat the oven to Gas Mark 4/180°C/fan oven 160°C. Heat a large non stick frying pan until hot, add the beef and stir fry over a high heat for about 5 minutes until browned. Add the onions, garlic, parsnip, carrots, ginger, lemon zest, garam masala and sultanas and then cook for 3–4 minutes until the vegetables are softened. Stir in the stock and simmer for 2–3 minutes.

2 Spoon the mixture into four individual ovenproof dishes (or follow the Tip if you prefer to use one dish), pressing it down firmly and smoothing the top. Place the dish on a baking tray.

3 In a jug, beat together the buttermilk, eggs and curry powder and season. Divide equally among the dishes and pour over the mince mixture. Share out the almonds between the dishes and scatter over. Bake for 20–25 minutes until set on top. Serve immediately.

cook's tip...

Make this in a 1.5 litre (2¾ pint) deep ovenproof dish and bake for 40 minutes until set.

make it fast

Even the most organised person sometimes needs to pull it out of the bag fast. That's when you need easy recipes like these – they're all ready in 30 minutes or less. Who would believe you could have a Creamy Chicken Pie or a Herby Smoked Salmon Frittata on the table so quickly – but you can. Rustle up tasty Mexican-style Tortillas with Refried Beans and Salsa in no time at all or spend just 5 minutes in the kitchen and enjoy a filling slice of Sausage and Onion Loaf less than half an hour later.

Mie goreng

Calories per serving 279　　　　Serves 4
Takes 15 mins

This lovely Indonesian dish is served with noodles.
Ketchap manis, or Indonesian ketchup, is widely available
in supermarkets and is a lovely sweet soy version of our
ketchup. Use it to spice up noodle and rice dishes or simply
as a condiment.

low fat cooking spray
1 egg, beaten
2 carrots, peeled and cut into thin strips
250 g (9 oz) mushrooms, sliced
110 g (4 oz) beansprouts
1 bunch of spring onions, chopped
320 g (11½ oz) medium straight to wok noodles
4 tablespoons ketchap manis
1 tablespoon light soy sauce
1 red pepper, de-seeded and cut
　　into thin strips
15 cm (6 inch) cucumber, cut into small cubes

1 Spray a wok or large non stick frying pan with the
cooking spray and heat until hot. Add the egg, swirling
it round the pan to make a thin omelette. Once set and
brown underneath, slide from the pan, cut into thin strips
and keep warm by covering with foil.

2 Spray the pan again and add the carrots and
mushrooms, stir frying over a high heat for about
3 minutes until the carrots have just softened. Add the
beansprouts and spring onions into the pan and cook
for a minute before adding the noodles. Warm through
and then stir in the ketchap manis and soy sauce.

3 Divide the stir fry between four bowls, top with
the pepper, cucumber and omelette strips and serve
immediately.

Turkey 'olives'

Calories per serving 328　　　　Serves 2
10 mins prep, 20 mins cooking
✳ **meat only**

2 × 125 g (4½ oz) turkey fillets, halved lengthways
　　but not quite all the way through
low fat cooking spray
150 ml (5 fl oz) chicken stock
300 g (10½ oz) new potatoes
75 g (2¾ oz) green beans
110 g (4 oz) broccoli

For the paste
25 g (1 oz) sun-dried tomatoes
about 300 ml (10 fl oz) boiling water
2 spring onions, chopped
25 g (1 oz) black olives in brine
½ teaspoon lemon zest

You will need cocktail sticks

1 Make the paste. Put the tomatoes in a small pan, pour
over enough boiling water to cover, bring to the boil
and simmer for 5 minutes. Drain and chop roughly. Put
the tomatoes and remaining paste ingredients in a food
processor, or use a hand held blender, and whizz to a
rough paste.

2 Place the turkey fillets between two sheets of cling film
and bash until 1 cm (½ inch) thick. Spread the paste over
one side of each piece of the turkey and roll up, securing
with a cocktail stick.

3 Spray a lidded non stick frying pan with the cooking
spray and heat until hot. Brown the turkey for 2–3 minutes
then pour over the stock. Cover and cook for 10 minutes
until tender.

4 Meanwhile, bring a pan of water to the boil, add the
potatoes and cook for 10–12 minutes, or until tender,
adding the beans and broccoli for the final 3 minutes. Serve
one turkey 'olive' each, sliced in half, with the potatoes and
vegetables alongside and the pan juices drizzled over.

Thai salmon rice

Calories per serving 416   **Serves 2**
Takes 30 mins

low fat cooking spray
2 shallots, chopped
2 teaspoons Thai 7 spice
80 g (3 oz) dried Thai or Jasmine rice
100 ml (3½ fl oz) light coconut milk
300 ml (10 fl oz) vegetable stock
150 g (5½ oz) green beans, trimmed and chopped
2 × 100 g (3½ oz) skinless salmon fillets

To serve
a handful of fresh coriander leaves
a lime, cut into wedges

1 Spray a large lidded pan with the cooking spray and heat until hot. Add the shallots and cook for 2 minutes. Stir in the Thai 7 spice and cook for a minute before adding the rice and stirring to coat. Pour over the coconut milk and stock, bring to the boil, cover and simmer for 2 minutes.

2 Stir in the beans and then place the salmon pieces on top of the rice. Cover and cook for 10–15 minutes until everything is cooked through.

3 Serve with the coriander sprinkled on top and the lime wedges on the side.

Try this Make this recipe with 125 g (4½ oz) haddock fillet instead of salmon.

cook's tip...

Thai 7 spice is a delicious combination of exotic spices and worth looking for since it's useful in stir fries as well as rice and noodle dishes.

Pasta with tomato pesto

Calories per serving 305   **Serves 4**
Takes 25 mins

You can whizz up the pesto in no time at all and it keeps well. Store it in the fridge for a few days or freeze it.

20 g (¾ oz) sun-dried tomatoes, cut into strips
about 300 ml (10 fl oz) boiling water
50 g (1¾ oz) pine nut kernels
200 g (7 oz) dried pasta shapes e.g. penne
2 teaspoons extra virgin olive oil
juice and zest of half a lemon
2 tablespoons chopped fresh parsley
8 cherry tomatoes, halved
2 handfuls of rocket leaves

1 Put the sun-dried tomatoes in a small pan, pour over enough boiling water to cover, bring to the boil and simmer for 5 minutes. Drain, reserving 2 tablespoons of the liquid.

2 Meanwhile, in a small frying pan, dry fry the pine nut kernels for 2–3 minutes, stirring regularly until golden.

3 Bring a large pan of water to the boil, add the pasta, and cook for 10–12 minutes or according to the packet instructions. Drain well and return to the pan.

4 In the meantime, place the soaked tomatoes and pine nut kernels in a small food processor or liquidiser and blend to a rough paste. Add the olive oil, lemon juice and zest and parsley. Blend again.

5 Toss the pesto into the pasta and stir through with the cherry tomatoes and reserved soaking liquid. Warm through over a low heat. Divide the pasta between warm bowls and serve with the rocket on top.

V **Try this** To give your pesto an extra kick, add ½ teaspoon of chilli flakes.

Sweet 'n' sticky pork

Calories per serving 299	**Serves 4**
Takes 30 mins	

The soy, honey and ginger go all sticky and tangy in the pan and make an incredibly delicious coating for the pork.

150 g (5½ oz) dried long grain rice
350 g (12 oz) pork tenderloin, visible fat
    removed, and cut into 12 slices
4 tablespoons soy sauce
2 tablespoons honey
1½ teaspoons grated fresh ginger
1 garlic clove, crushed
a pinch of chilli flakes (optional)
low fat cooking spray
2 carrots, peeled and cut into thin sticks
150 g (5½ oz) mange tout or sugar snap peas

1 Bring a pan of water to the boil, add the rice and cook for 10–12 minutes or according to the packet instructions. Drain and keep warm.

2 Meanwhile, lay the pork slices on a board and cover with a sheet of cling film. Bash with the end of a rolling pin until about 1 cm (½ inch) thick.

3 In a shallow bowl, mix together the soy, honey, ginger, garlic and chilli, if using. Spray a large non stick frying pan with the cooking spray and heat until hot. Dip the pork pieces into the soy mixture and add to the pan, cooking for a couple of minutes, before turning and cooking the underside. You may need to do this in batches. The pork should be dark and sticky and cooked through. Add any left over soy mixture to the pan to warm through.

4 Meanwhile, bring a small pan of water to the boil, add the carrots and cook for 3 minutes before adding the mange tout or sugar snap peas and cooking for a further 2 minutes until tender.

5 Serve the pork on a pile of rice with any pan juices drizzled over and the vegetables on the side.

Try this This sticky sauce works well with four 125 g (4½ oz) turkey fillets instead of the pork.

Redcurrant duck with pasta

Calories per serving 441	Serves 2
Takes 30 mins	

The gamey flavour of duck is especially good with redcurrant sauce. Serve with a salad of rocket, spinach and cherry tomatoes, drizzled with a little balsamic vinegar, instead of the broccoli and beans.

low fat cooking spray
2 × 130 g (4¾ oz) skinless, boneless duck breasts
2 teaspoons soy sauce
1 tablespoon redcurrant jelly
125 g (4½ oz) dried tagliatelle
125 g (4½ oz) tenderstem broccoli
75 g (2¾ oz) green beans, trimmed

1 Preheat the oven to Gas Mark 6/200°C/fan oven 180°C. Spray a non stick frying pan with cooking spray and heat until hot. Add the duck breasts and brown all over, cooking for about 5 minutes. Place on a non stick baking tray.

2 Add the soy sauce and redcurrant jelly to the frying pan and warm through. Brush the mixture over the duck breasts and place in the oven for 10–15 minutes or until firm to the touch. Reserve any juices.

3 In the meantime, bring a large pan of water to the boil, add the pasta and cook according to the packet instructions. Add the broccoli and beans 3–4 minutes before the end of cooking and cook until just tender. Drain and serve with the duck and any remaining pan juices.

Try this This recipe works equally well with two 125 g (4½ oz) skinless, boneless chicken breasts.

Lamb steaks with red mojo sauce

Calories per serving 199	Serves 4
Takes 25 mins	

Mojo sauce comes from the Canaries but versions are found in the Caribbean too. It's great with grilled meats and meaty fish such as tuna. Serve with 125 g (4½ oz) cooked potatoes per person.

4 × 110 g (4 oz) lamb leg steaks, visible fat removed
2 teaspoons cumin seeds
1 teaspoon paprika
2 red peppers, de-seeded and chopped roughly
2 garlic cloves, chopped roughly
2 tablespoons red wine vinegar
1 tablespoon extra virgin olive oil
150 g bag spinach and watercress salad, to serve
salt and freshly ground black pepper

You will need a mortar and pestle or a rolling pin and chopping board

1 Preheat the grill to medium and line the grill pan with foil. Season the steaks on both sides and grill for 10–15 minutes turning once or twice, until browned.

2 Meanwhile, dry fry the cumin seeds in a small pan until aromatic. Roughly crush in a mortar and pestle or use the end of a rolling pin on a chopping board. Place all the remaining ingredients, except the olive oil and spinach and watercress salad, in a liquidiser, or use a hand held blender, and blend until smooth. Add the olive oil and blend again.

3 Serve the steaks with the sauce on top and the spinach and watercress salad on the side.

Quick beef stew

Calories per serving 314   Serves 4
Takes 30 mins
❄ stew only

You can easily double this recipe and freeze half for an instant meal another time.

600 g (1 lb 5 oz) potatoes, peeled and chopped
low fat cooking spray
350 g (12 oz) lean frying steak, cut into thin strips
1 large onion, sliced
1 red pepper, de-seeded and sliced
1 yellow pepper, de-seeded and sliced
50 ml (2 fl oz) red wine
400 g can chopped tomatoes with herbs
300 ml (10 fl oz) beef stock
60 g (2 oz) pitted black olives in brine,
    drained and halved
salt and freshly ground black pepper

1 Bring a lidded pan of water to the boil, add the potatoes, cover and cook for 10–15 minutes until tender. Drain well, season and mash. Keep warm.

2 Meanwhile, spray a large non stick frying pan with the cooking spray and heat until hot. Add the steak and stir fry for 3 minutes until just brown. Remove from the pan and set aside.

3 Spray the frying pan again, add the onion and peppers and stir fry for 3–5 minutes until softened, adding a little water if they begin to stick. Add the wine, letting it sizzle and subside before adding the tomatoes, stock and olives. Bring to the boil and simmer for 5 minutes. Return the meat to the pan and cook for a further 2–3 minutes until hot. Serve the stew with the mash.

Try this If you prefer, use a can of plain chopped tomatoes and add a teaspoon of mixed dried herbs.

Herby smoked salmon frittata

Calories per serving 261   Serves 4
Takes 30 mins

Make this for supper or enjoy it cold the next day. Serve with some watercress and cherry tomatoes, with lemon juice squeezed over.

350 g (12 oz) new potatoes, halved if large
2 tablespoons chopped fresh parsley
1 tablespoon chopped fresh dill
6 eggs, beaten
low fat cooking spray
120 g pack smoked salmon, cut into strips
freshly ground black pepper

You will need a large, grill proof, non stick frying pan (see Cook's tip)

1 Bring a large lidded pan of water to the boil and add the potatoes. Bring back to the boil, cover and simmer for 10 minutes until just tender. Drain and rinse in cold water. Once cool enough to handle, slice thinly.

2 Mix the herbs into the eggs and season with black pepper. Spray the non stick frying pan with the cooking spray and heat until hot. Add the potatoes, then pour in the egg. Scatter over the smoked salmon pieces and cook gently for 5–10 minutes until set. Meanwhile, preheat the grill to medium.

3 Place the pan under the grill to brown the top. Serve hot or warm in wedges.

cook's tip...

If you don't have a grill proof frying pan, carefully slide the cooked frittata from the pan on to a baking sheet sprayed with the cooking spray and grill.

Tortillas with refried beans and salsa

Calories per serving 458   Serves 2

Takes 25 mins

'Refried' comes from the Mexican word 'refritos' meaning 'well fried' and refers to the process of cooking the beans in a frying pan, which makes them taste especially yummy.

low fat cooking spray

1 red onion, sliced

1 green pepper, de-seeded and chopped

1 garlic clove, crushed

410 g can borlotti beans, drained

400 g can chopped tomatoes

1 teaspoon smoked paprika

a pinch of dried chilli flakes

2 × 75 g (2¾ oz) soft flour wraps

For the salsa

6 cherry tomatoes, quartered

2 spring onions, sliced

finely grated zest and juice of a lime

2 tablespoons reduced fat soured cream

1   Spray a non stick frying pan with the cooking spray and heat until hot. Add the onion and pepper and stir fry for 5 minutes. Add the garlic and cook for a further minute. Add the beans, tomatoes, paprika and chilli flakes to the pan and leave to a gentle simmer for 10 minutes until slightly thickened. Mash the beans lightly with a masher or fork to thicken further but leave about half of them whole.

2   To make the salsa, combine the tomatoes, spring onions, lime zest and juice and set aside for 5 minutes. Preheat the grill to medium.

3   Warm the wraps under the grill for a minute and then divide the bean mixture between the two. Add a dollop of the salsa and the soured cream and roll up to form a cone. Serve immediately.

Ⓥ Try this   Pinto beans or kidney beans work just as well as borlotti beans.

If you have time, cook the beans in step 1 and then leave them for a couple of hours to allow the flavours to develop and intensify.

Tasty, fresh and filling, these tortillas will leave you feeling satisfied.

Creamy chicken pies

Calories per serving 481   Serves 2

Takes 30 mins

400 g (14 oz) potatoes, peeled and cut into
    small chunks

125 g (4½ oz) parsnip, peeled and cut into
    small chunks

300 g (10½ oz) skinless, boneless chicken
    breasts, cut into small chunks

1 carrot, peeled and sliced thinly

250 ml (9 fl oz) hot chicken stock

1 bay leaf

60 g (2 oz) sweetcorn, frozen or canned

2 teaspoons cornflour

40 g (1½ oz) low fat soft cheese

1 tablespoon chopped fresh parsley

salt and freshly ground black pepper

You will need two individual pie or gratin dishes
or a 750 ml (1¼ pint) ovenproof dish

1   Bring a lidded pan of water to the boil. Add the
potatoes and parsnips. Cover and simmer for 10 minutes
until soft. Drain well and mash with a little seasoning.

2   Meanwhile, place the chicken, carrot, stock and bay
leaf in a medium sized pan. Bring to the boil and simmer,
uncovered, for 5 minutes. Add the sweetcorn and bring
back to the boil.

3   Mix the cornflour with 1 tablespoon of water, then stir
to a paste. Stir the cornflour paste into the chicken mixture
and let the mixture bubble for a minute before whisking in
the soft cheese and cooking gently for a minute or so until
hot. Remove the bay leaf. Stir in the parsley. Preheat the
grill to medium.

4   Spoon the chicken mixture into individual pie or gratin
dishes or the ovenproof dish and top with the mash. Grill
for 3–5 minutes until the potato is just golden on the top.
Serve immediately.

Sausage and onion loaf

Calories per serving 294   Serves 4

5 mins prep, 25 mins cooking

This speedy version of meatloaf freezes very well. Serve it
in slices with a salad of Little Gem lettuce, cherry tomatoes,
cucumber and apple slices.

450 g pack Weight Watchers Premium Pork
    Sausages

110 g (4 oz) fresh breadcrumbs

1 onion, sliced very thinly

1 large carrot, peeled and grated

2 tablespoons chopped fresh parsley

8 fresh sage leaves, chopped

low fat cooking spray

freshly ground black pepper

You will need a 900 g (2 lb) loaf tin

1   Preheat the oven to Gas Mark 6/200°C/fan oven 180°C.
Squeeze the sausage meat from the skins into a large bowl.
Mix in the breadcrumbs, vegetables and herbs – it's easiest
to do this with your hands. Season with some black pepper.

2   Spray the loaf tin with the cooking spray and then
press the mixture into the tin. Bake for 20–25 minutes until
beginning to brown on the top. Serve in slices.

cook's tip...

This is delicious cold too so it's ideal to enjoy as a
lunch at work or on a picnic.

eating out
at home

Eating out at home is increasingly popular and it's fun to discover how to enjoy your favourite 'eating out' dishes at home with friends and family. You can take your time and savour a takeaway meal surrounded by your home comforts, knowing it's much better for you than the local Indian. Fantastic. Now there's no need to rely on pub grub for a lovely Beef and Ale Pot Pie or the local chippy for a delicious Butterflied Garlic Chicken. Simply dip into this chapter, relax and enjoy.

Prawn nachos on page 122

Lentil burgers with raita

Calories per serving 450 **Serves 4**
15 mins prep + 30 mins chilling, 30 mins cooking

1 onion, chopped roughly
2 garlic cloves, peeled
1 teaspoon ground coriander
½ teaspoon ground cumin
410 g can lentils, drained
125 g (4½ oz) fresh breadcrumbs
a handful of chopped fresh coriander leaves
low fat cooking spray
3 tablespoons low fat plain yogurt
2 teaspoons chopped fresh mint
10 cm (4 inch) cucumber, grated
4 × 80 g (3 oz) crusty bread rolls
½ small Iceberg lettuce, torn
2 tomatoes, sliced

1 Preheat the oven to Gas Mark 6/200˚C/fan oven 180˚C. Put the onion in a food processor or use a hand held blender. Whizz until chopped. Add the garlic, spices, lentils, breadcrumbs and coriander. Whizz again to a thick rough paste. Shape into four burgers and chill for 30 minutes.
2 Spray a baking sheet with the cooking spray. Place the burgers on it, spray the tops and bake for 30 minutes until beginning to brown.
3 Mix together the yogurt, mint and cucumber. To serve the burgers, split the crusty rolls, top with the lettuce, a burger each and the tomatoes then divide the yogurt mixture between them. Serve immediately.

cook's tip...

 To freeze, put baking parchment between the uncooked burgers and store them in a container. To cook from frozen, add an extra 10–15 minutes.

Bang bang chicken

Calories per serving 505 **Serves 2**
10 mins prep, 15 mins cooking

This is a lighter version of a Szechuan dish which normally has a very heavy peanut sauce. Serve it with a cucumber salad: cut ribbons of cucumber, lay on a plate, sprinkle with salt and leave to drain for 5 minutes. Rinse and pat dry before serving alongside the chicken.

2 × 140 g (5 oz) skinless, boneless chicken
    breasts, halved into two long pieces
500 ml (18 fl oz) chicken stock
1 piece lemon grass, tough outer stalks removed,
    halved lengthways
1 teaspoon roughly chopped fresh ginger
2 garlic cloves, crushed
1 red chilli, halved and de-seeded
125 g (4½ oz) dried fine rice noodles
2 heads pak choi, leaves separated
60 g (2 oz) baby corn
20 g (¾ oz) roasted unsalted peanuts, crushed
a handful of fresh coriander leaves, to serve

1 Place the chicken pieces in a shallow, lidded pan and pour over the stock. Add the lemon grass, ginger, garlic and one piece of the chilli. Bring to the boil, cover and simmer gently for 10 minutes until cooked through. Remove from the pan and keep warm.
2 Add the noodles, pak choi and baby corn to the pan and simmer gently, uncovered for 5 minutes.
3 Finely dice the remaining chilli. Serve the noodles and vegetables in a shallow bowl topped with the chicken pieces, peanuts, chilli and coriander.

Mushroom galettes

Calories per serving 215 **Serves 4**
Takes 35 mins

The galette is a savoury French pancake, most commonly served in Brittany and Normandy, and made from buckwheat flour.

75 g (2¾ oz) buckwheat flour
1 egg
200 ml (7 fl oz) skimmed milk
1 teaspoon sunflower oil
low fat cooking spray
700 g (1 lb 9 oz) mixed mushrooms
   e.g. chestnut, button, field, sliced
2 garlic cloves, crushed
1 tablespoon fresh thyme leaves or
   1 teaspoon dried
1 tablespoon Marsala wine
60 g (2 oz) Gruyère cheese, grated

1 Place the flour in a large bowl and make a well in the middle. Crack the egg into the well (it's easier to crack it into a small bowl first) and begin stirring with a wooden spoon, gradually drawing in the flour. Once the mixture is too thick to stir, add the milk a little at a time until you have a smooth batter. Leave to stand for 5 minutes.

2 Heat the oil in a large non stick frying pan until hot. Tip out any excess oil into a ramekin. Add a ladleful of batter and swirl around the pan to coat. Cook for 2 minutes until golden underneath. Flip the galette and cook the other side for about a minute until golden. Slide out of the pan on to a plate and repeat to make three more pancakes, layering the cooked pancakes with greaseproof paper and covering with foil to keep them warm.

3 Wipe out the pan and spray with the cooking spray. Heat until hot then add the mushrooms and cook for 5 minutes. Add the garlic and thyme. The mushrooms will release their juices and, once they have evaporated, will begin to brown. At this point, add the Marsala wine and then let it bubble and almost disappear before removing from the heat.

4 Preheat the grill to medium. Line the grill pan with foil. Place a galette on the grill pan and top with a quarter of the mushrooms, fold the galette over, top with the cheese and grill to melt. Carefully slide the galette on to a serving plate and keep warm while you make the others. Repeat to make three more. Serve hot.

V Try this Instead of Marsala wine, use a tablespoonful of brandy.

Get ahead by making these pancakes the day before and then warm them through under the grill.

Use buckwheat flour in breads and other pancakes such as Scotch pancakes or blinis for a lovely nutty flavour.

Thai pork with egg fried rice

Calories per serving 345	**Serves 2**
Takes 20 mins	

If you have time, leave the pork to marinate for 20 minutes but if not, even 5 minutes will give you lots of extra flavour.

200 g (7 oz) lean pork fillet, visible fat removed, and sliced thinly
2 teaspoons green Thai curry paste
80 g (3 oz) dried Thai or Jasmine rice
low fat cooking spray
6 spring onions, sliced
1 red pepper, de-seeded and diced
110 g (4 oz) baby corn, halved
1 egg
finely grated zest and juice of ½ a lime
salt
a handful of fresh coriander leaves, to garnish

1 Place the pork slices in a bowl and stir in the Thai paste with a pinch of salt. Set aside for 5 minutes.
2 Bring a large pan of water to the boil, add the rice and cook for 10–12 minutes until tender, or according to the packet instructions. Drain really well and set aside.
3 Spray a wok or large non stick frying pan with the cooking spray and heat until hot. Add the pork and cook for 2–3 minutes, turning until beginning to brown. Add the vegetables and stir fry for 2–3 minutes.
4 Spray another frying pan with the cooking spray and heat until hot. Add the rice and stir fry for a minute or so to drive off any excess water. Push the rice to one side of the pan, add the egg and quickly scramble it – a chopstick is great for this. Then bring the rice in and continue stir frying until hot. Remove from the heat and stir in the lime zest and juice. Serve with the pork, garnish with the coriander.

Butterflied garlic chicken

Calories per serving 238	**Serves 4**
10 mins prep, 20 mins cooking	

You can serve the chicken with a large salad made with Iceberg lettuce, shredded, cucumber, cut into batons, red pepper, de-seeded and cut into thin strips, celery stick, chopped and cherry tomatoes, halved.

low fat cooking spray
50 g (1¾ oz) dried polenta
1 garlic clove, crushed
1 tablespoon mixed dried herbs
1 egg
4 × 125 g (4½ oz) skinless, boneless chicken breasts
salt and freshly ground black pepper

1 Preheat the oven to Gas Mark 6/200°C/fan oven 180°C. Spray a baking tray with the cooking spray. Mix together the polenta, garlic and mixed herbs in a shallow bowl and add seasoning. Beat the egg in a separate shallow bowl.
2 Carefully cut horizontally into each chicken breast, ensuring you don't cut all the way through, so that when you open it out you have a butterfly shape.
3 Dip the chicken first into the egg and then the polenta mix. Place on the baking sheet and bake for 15–20 minutes until golden and the chicken is cooked through. Serve hot.

Try this Enjoy with the same quantities of turkey fillets instead of chicken.

Beef and ale pot pies

Calories per serving 304   **Serves 4**
15 mins prep, 1 hr 20 mins cooking

During cooking, the ale in these really meaty pies creates a wonderful aroma. They're filling but you could also serve them with 150 g (5½ oz) potatoes per person, boiled and mashed.

2 tablespoons plain flour
400 g (14 oz) lean braising steak, cubed
low fat cooking spray
1 large onion, chopped
2 garlic cloves, sliced
2 carrots, peeled and chopped
250 g (9 oz) swede, chopped
250 ml (9 fl oz) brown ale
250 ml (9 fl oz) beef stock
1 bay leaf
2 × 45 g (1½ oz) sheets filo pastry, measuring
    50 × 24 cm (20 × 9½ inches), defrosted if frozen
salt and freshly ground black pepper

You will need four gratin dishes or large ramekins

1 Place the flour on a large plate and season. Toss the beef cubes in the flour. Remove to a plate, shaking off any excess.

2 Spray a large lidded pan with the cooking spray and heat until hot. Add the beef and cook over a high heat until browned all over. Remove from the pan and set aside. Spray the pan again, add the onion, garlic, carrots and swede and stir fry for 5 minutes until beginning to brown.

3 Add the ale, letting it sizzle up, then add the stock, bay leaf and the beef. Bring to the boil, cover and leave to gently simmer for 40 minutes, stirring occasionally. Remove the lid. Simmer for another 20 minutes until the meat is really tender.

4 Preheat the oven to Gas Mark 6/200°C/fan oven 180°C. Remove the bay leaf and divide the beef between four gratin dishes or large ramekins. Cut each sheet of pastry in half and then spray with the cooking spray. Scrunch up the pastry on top of each pie to cover and spray again with the cooking spray. Bake in the oven for 20 minutes until the pastry is golden. Serve immediately.

Prawn nachos

Calories per serving 466	Serves 2
25 mins prep, 20 mins cooking	

3 pitta breads (about 160 g/5¾ oz total)
low fat cooking spray
1 teaspoon smoked paprika
1 large onion, sliced
1 garlic clove, crushed
1 red chilli, de-seeded and diced finely
1 green pepper, de-seeded and sliced
1 red pepper, de-seeded and sliced
400 g can chopped tomatoes
175 g (6 oz) cooked and peeled prawns,
    defrosted if frozen
2 tablespoons chopped fresh parsley
25 g (1 oz) half fat Cheddar cheese, grated
10 cm (4 inch) cucumber, diced
2 tablespoons 0% fat Greek yogurt

You will need a heatproof platter

1 Preheat the oven to Gas Mark 4/180°C/fan oven 160°C. To make the chips, split each pitta bread into two pieces. Cut each piece into six triangles to make 36 triangles in all. Put them on a baking sheet and spray with the cooking spray. Sprinkle over the paprika. Bake for 5 minutes until crispy and starting to brown. Remove from the oven.

2 Spray a large non stick frying pan with the cooking spray and heat until hot. Add the onion and cook, stirring for 3 minutes, then add the garlic, chilli, peppers and a little water to stop them sticking. Cook for 5 minutes until softened then add the tomatoes. Reduce the heat to a gentle simmer and cook for 20 minutes until thickened.

3 Preheat the grill to medium. Stir the prawns and parsley into the sauce. Heat through for a minute. Arrange the chips on a heatproof platter, top with the prawn sauce and scatter over the cheese. Grill for a couple of minutes .

4 Mix the cucumber into the yogurt. Serve on the side.

Moules Provençales

Calories per serving 697	Serves 2
Takes 35 mins	

Mussels are in season over the colder months, roughly from September to April (months with an 'r' in them). They make a delicious economical treat.

1 kg (2 lb 4 oz) mussels in their shells
low fat cooking spray
1 large onion, sliced
2 garlic cloves, sliced
150 ml (5 fl oz) dry white wine
150 ml (5 fl oz) fish or vegetable stock
3 tomatoes on the vine, chopped
1 fresh thyme sprig
1 fresh rosemary sprig
1 lemon, cut into wedges
1 tablespoon chopped fresh parsley, to garnish
140 g (5 oz) baguette, halved, to serve

1 Place the mussels in a large bowl of cold water and scrub them clean, removing any barnacles and pulling out the beards (the weedy bit that sticks out). Drain.

2 Spray a large, lidded non stick pan with the cooking spray and heat until hot. Add the onions and sauté for 5 minutes until softened. Add the garlic and cook for a minute before adding the wine. Let it bubble for a minute then pour in the stock and add the tomatoes, thyme and rosemary. Simmer for 5 minutes, allowing the tomatoes to soften then tip in the mussels. Cover and let them cook for 5–7 minutes.

3 During this time, most of the shells should open but any that have not should be discarded. Spoon the mussels into large warmed bowls and serve with the sauce, lemon wedges and parsley. Serve a piece of baguette each for mopping up the delicious juices.

Try using an empty shell to pry each tasty mussel from its shell – it's the traditional way and helps you to savour each one.

Chilli lamb sambal

Calories per serving 333	Serves 4
15 mins prep, 35 mins cooking	

Sambal, from Indonesia and Malaysia, is a versatile sauce used for main meals or as an accompaniment. This version is mild but if you can take the heat, increase the chilli.

1 shallot, chopped
1 red chilli, de-seeded and chopped roughly
½ stick lemon grass, outer stalks removed
    and chopped
2 teaspoons tamarind paste
1 teaspoon turmeric
1 teaspoon sugar
low fat cooking spray
600 g (1 lb 5 oz) sweet potatoes, peeled
    and cut into wedges
4 × 150 g (5½ oz) leg lamb steaks,
    visible fat removed
1 cucumber, cut into ribbons
16 cherry tomatoes, halved

1 Place the shallot, chilli and lemon grass in a food processor, or use a hand held blender, and whizz to chop. Add the tamarind paste, turmeric and sugar. Whizz to a rough paste.
2 Preheat the oven to Gas Mark 5/190°C/fan oven 170°C. Spray a small non stick frying pan with the cooking spray and heat until hot. Add the paste and cook for 2–3 minutes to soften the shallot and cook the spices. If it gets too dry, add 1 or 2 tablespoons of water.
3 Put the sweet potatoes in a roasting tin and spray with the cooking spray. Roast for 15 minutes then add the lamb steaks, spreading the paste over them. Roast for 15–20 minutes until the meat is cooked and the potatoes tender.
4 Serve the meat and wedges with the cucumber and tomatoes on the side.

Jamaican pork with rice 'n' beans

Calories per serving 612	Serves 2
Takes 30 mins	

This straightforward dish is full of flavours that work incredibly well together.

227 g can pineapple rings in natural juice,
    drained, reserving 2 tablespoons of juice
2 tablespoons Jerk spices
2 × 150 g (5½ oz) lean pork loin steaks, visible fat
    removed
80 g (3 oz) dried long grain rice
400 g can black beans, drained
1 tablespoon chopped fresh coriander
salt and freshly ground black pepper

1 Preheat the oven to Gas Mark 5/190°C/fan oven 170°C. Place two pineapple rings in the base of a small ovenproof dish. Mix together the reserved pineapple juice and the Jerk spices to a paste. Smear the paste over both sides of the steaks and sit on top of the pineapple. Set aside to marinate for 10 minutes.
2 Bake the pork for 15–20 minutes until just cooked through.
3 Meanwhile, bring a large lidded pan of water to the boil, add the rice and cook for 10–12 minutes or according to the packet instructions. Drain, stir in the beans, cover and leave for 5 minutes until the beans have warmed through. Stir through the coriander and season.
4 Serve the pork steaks with a pineapple ring each and the rice with any juices spooned over.

Try this If you can't find black beans, use the same quantity of pinto beans instead.

Cheesy mushroom tarts

Calories per serving 192   Serves 2
20 mins prep, 10 mins cooking

Serve with a crunchy lettuce and watercress salad with some balsamic vinegar drizzled over.

low fat cooking spray
300 g (10½ oz) mixed mushrooms, sliced
a bunch of spring onions, sliced
1 fresh rosemary sprig, chopped
60 g (2 oz) low fat soft cheese with garlic and herbs
45 g (1½ oz) sheet filo pastry, measuring 50 × 24 cm
    (20 × 9½ inches), defrosted if frozen
50 g (1¾ oz) reduced fat feta cheese
freshly ground black pepper

1 Preheat the oven to Gas Mark 6/200°C/fan oven 180°C. Spray a large non stick frying pan with the cooking spray, add the mushrooms and cook over a high heat for 5 minutes. Add the onions and rosemary then continue cooking until the mushrooms have released their juices and they have evaporated.

2 Remove from the heat and stir in the soft cheese so that it forms a sauce. Season with black pepper.

3 Lay the pastry sheet on a board and spray with the cooking spray. Cut the pastry into four squares. Spray a baking sheet with the cooking spray, layer two pastry squares on top of each other and place on the baking sheet, to make two piles in total. Spoon the mushrooms into the centre of the filo squares and scrunch up the edges. Spray with the cooking spray, crumble over the feta cheese and bake for 10 minutes until golden.

Moroccan salad

Calories per serving 290   Serves 2
20 mins prep, 30 mins cooking

Roast the potatoes the night before and you'll have a delicious take-to-work lunch.

low fat cooking spray
250 g (9 oz) sweet potatoes, peeled and
    cut into wedges
15 g (½ oz) harissa paste
1 tablespoon coriander seeds, crushed roughly
15 g (½ oz) sunflower seeds
1 Cos lettuce, leaves divided
a handful of rocket leaves
4 tomatoes on the vine, quartered
1 celery stick, sliced
1 yellow pepper, de-seeded and sliced
25 g (1 oz) raisins
1 tablespoon white wine vinegar
1 tablespoon chopped fresh mint

1 Preheat the oven to Gas Mark 6/200°C/fan oven 180°C. Line a baking tray with foil and spray with the cooking spray. In a bowl, coat the potato wedges with 2 teaspoons of the harissa paste. Once coated, place them on the baking tray and sprinkle with the coriander seeds. Roast for 20–30 minutes until tender and beginning to brown.

2 Heat a small non stick frying pan and dry fry the sunflower seeds for 1–2 minutes until they begin to pop and turn brown. Remove from the heat and set aside.

3 Divide the lettuce and rocket between two serving plates. Top with the tomatoes, celery, pepper and raisins. Mix together the remainder of the harissa paste, vinegar and mint.

4 Arrange the potato wedges on top of the salad and drizzle with the dressing. Scatter over the sunflower seeds and serve.

Italian pork parcels

Calories per serving 352	**Serves 4**
Takes 50 mins	
❋ **for parcels and sauce**	

Pork goes so well with peppers and fennel in these parcels and the peppadew peppers add a delicious piquancy and touch of heat.

low fat cooking spray

1 yellow pepper, de-seeded and diced

1 onion, diced

1 small fennel bulb, diced

300 g (10½ oz) lean pork mince

4 peppadew peppers, drained and sliced

1 teaspoon dried oregano

4 tablespoons chicken stock

20 g (¾ oz) green pitted olives in brine,
      drained and sliced

4 × 45 g (1½ oz) sheets filo pastry,
      measuring 50 × 24 cm (20 × 9½ inches),
      defrosted if frozen

300 g pack green beans, trimmed, to serve

For the sauce

450 g (1 lb) tomatoes, chopped roughly

½ teaspoon sugar

2 fresh thyme sprigs

1 bay leaf

2 tablespoons chicken or vegetable stock

1 Spray a large non stick frying pan with the cooking spray and heat until hot. Add the pepper, onion and fennel and cook for 5 minutes until softened. Add the pork mince and cook for 2–3 minutes until browned. Stir in the peppadews, oregano, stock and olives. Reduce the heat and simmer gently for 5 minutes.

2 Preheat the oven to Gas Mark 6/200°C/fan oven 180°C. Cut the filo sheets in half to make eight squares then layer up two squares spraying each with the cooking spray. Spoon the mixture into the middle of the squares and fold up the sides to form a parcel. Spray a baking tray with the cooking spray and transfer the parcel. Repeat to make four parcels in total. Spray the parcels with the cooking spray then bake for 10–15 minutes until golden.

3 To make the sauce, place all the ingredients in a pan, bring to the boil and leave to simmer gently for 10–15 minutes until pulpy. Remove the bay leaf and any twiggy bits of thyme, then blend using a hand held blender or transfer to a liquidiser to blend until smooth.

4 Meanwhile, bring a small pan of water to the boil, add the beans and cook for 3–5 minutes until just tender. Serve a parcel each with the beans and tomato sauce spooned over.

food
to impress

It can sometimes be a challenge to stick to your weight loss plan while entertaining friends and family, so we've created a great selection of new recipes just for that – for sharing while you stay on track. These recipes are sure to be a hit – impress your guests with the Spanish Pork Pie or dish up the aromatic Lamb Tagine and don't be surprised when everyone asks for the recipe.

Cider braised stuffed chicken

Calories per serving 367	Serves 2
20 mins prep, 30 mins cooking	
❄	

White breadcrumbs work well in this recipe if you have them to hand, but wholemeal adds a good nutty flavour. Serve with 150 g (5½ oz) carrots, chopped, 100 g (4½ oz) peas, boiled, as well as 125 g (4½ oz) potatoes, mashed with 30 ml (1 fl oz) of skimmed milk each.

2 × 150 g (5½ oz) skinless, boneless
   chicken breasts
low fat cooking spray
1 red onion, cut into thin slices
150 ml (5 fl oz) dry cider
freshly ground black pepper

For the stuffing
50 g (1¾ oz) wholemeal breadcrumbs
2 teaspoons capers in brine
4 fresh sage leaves, chopped
1 garlic clove, diced
15 g (½ oz) low fat spread

1 Place the chicken breasts between two sheets of cling film on a chopping board and bash gently with the end of a rolling pin to flatten slightly. Use a sharp knife to cut into the meat to form a pocket.

2 Mix together the ingredients for the stuffing and season with some black pepper. Push the stuffing into the pocket, pulling the chicken over. Keep back about a tablespoon of the mixture.

3 Preheat the oven to Gas Mark 4/180°C/fan oven 160°C. Spray a non stick frying pan with the cooking spray and heat until hot. Add the onion and cook, stirring occasionally for 5 minutes until softened. Spoon into an ovenproof dish which will hold the chicken snugly.

4 Place the chicken on top of the onions and pour over the cider. Scatter over the remaining stuffing. Spray a sheet of foil with the cooking spray and cover the dish. Bake for 20 minutes, then remove the foil and cook for a further 10 minutes until the chicken is cooked through. Serve immediately.

cook's tip...

To make fresh breadcrumbs, put the bread in a food processor or use a hand held blender and whizz it to crumbs. Alternatively, use a grater to grate the bread into crumbs.

Sea bass
with caper sauce

Calories per serving 298	Serves 4
Takes 30 mins	

Serve with 150 g (5½ oz) each of steamed baby carrots and leeks.

low fat cooking spray
450 g (1 lb) potatoes, peeled and diced
4 × 150 g (5½ oz) sea bass fillets, skin left on
400 g (14 oz) spinach, rinsed
salt and freshly ground black pepper

For the caper sauce
150 g pot 0% fat Greek yogurt
2 tablespoons capers in brine, drained
    and chopped roughly
finely grated zest of a lemon, then cut the lemon
    into wedges, to serve

1 Spray a large non stick frying pan with the cooking spray and heat until hot. Add the potatoes and stir fry for about 10–15 minutes, allowing them to brown and cook through. Remove from the pan and keep warm.

2 Wipe out the pan and spray again with the cooking spray. Add the fish fillets skin side down and cook for 2–3 minutes until crispy. Turn and cook the top side for about 2 minutes until cooked through. Remove to a plate and keep warm.

3 Put the spinach in a large lidded saucepan and cook for a minute or so until wilted. There's no need to add any water since there will be enough clinging to the leaves from the rinsing. Drain well and season.

4 For the caper sauce, put the yogurt in a small pan and warm through very gently. Don't let it boil or it will split. Stir in the capers and lemon zest.

5 Serve the sea bass on a pile of crisp potatoes, with the spinach alongside, topped with the sauce and a wedge of lemon for squeezing over.

Sophisticated sea bass, with its rich and satisfying flavour, is ideal for a special meal.

Sweet potato and carrot fritters

Calories per serving 141   Serves 4

Takes 20 mins

Serve these tasty fritters as a starter or with 50 g (1¾ oz) sliced tomatoes on the vine and 50 g (1¾ oz) soda bread each for a lovely lunch.

300 g (10½ oz) sweet potatoes, peeled and grated coarsely
140 g (5 oz) carrots, peeled and grated coarsely
2 eggs, beaten
2 teaspoons cumin seeds
low fat cooking spray
salt and freshly ground black pepper

To serve
150 g (5½ oz) watercress
4 teaspoons reduced fat soured cream

1 Mix together the potatoes and carrots with a little seasoning. Stir in the eggs and cumin seeds.

2 Spray a large non stick frying pan with the cooking spray and heat until hot. Add spoonfuls of the mixture, pressing down with a spatula to flatten. Cook for about 5 minutes turning once or twice until browned and cooked through. Remove to a plate and keep warm, either in the oven or by covering with foil while you make the remainder.

3 Serve two fritters each, arranged on a bed of watercress with the soured cream on the top.

Harissa chick peas

Calories per serving 243   Serves 2

Takes 15 mins

This elegant starter or light meal is lovely served straight away, slightly warm. However, serve cold, if you prefer.

low fat cooking spray
1 red onion, sliced thinly
1 courgette, diced
4 teaspoons harissa
400 g can chick peas, drained
4 tablespoons 0% fat Greek yogurt

To serve
Little Gem leaves
3 radishes, quartered
½ cucumber, cut into ribbons

1 Spray a non stick frying pan with the cooking spray and heat until hot. Add the onion and courgette and cook for 5 minutes until softened. You may need to add a splash of water if they start to stick. Add the harissa and cook for another 2–3 minutes. Remove from the heat.

2 Stir in the chick peas and yogurt.

3 Serve the chick pea mixture with the salad leaves, radishes and cucumber on the side.

cook's tip...

Harissa is a north African paste usually made from chillies, tomatoes and paprika but the ingredients do vary regionally. Smear it over meat or vegetables before cooking for extra flavour.

Crushed beans with mint and feta

Calories per serving 127	Serves 4
Takes 15 mins	

This makes a lovely starter. Use fresh broad beans in season, boiled for 3–4 minutes until tender.

130 g (4¾ oz) baguette
110 g (4 oz) frozen broad beans, defrosted and
    slipped from their outer grey skins before cooking
finely grated zest of ½ a lemon
50 g (1¾ oz) light feta cheese
1 tablespoon shredded fresh mint leaves, plus a
    couple of extra leaves, to garnish
freshly ground black pepper

1 Preheat the grill to medium. Slice the baguette in half lengthways and then in two again so you have four pieces. Toast the cut sides for a minute or so until golden.
2 Meanwhile, mix the beans, lemon zest, feta and mint together roughly, crushing everything together. Season with some black pepper.
3 Top the toasts with the bean mixture and serve garnished with some mint leaves.

ⓥ Try this Make this recipe using 110 g (4 oz) peas, defrosted if frozen, instead of beans.

cook's tip...

> You could prepare the bean mixture up to 1 hour ahead then cover and chill until required.

Chinese spiced beef casserole

Calories per serving 270	Serves 4
20 mins prep, 1 hr cooking	

This slow cooked beef, with a hint of ginger and Chinese five spice, just melts in the mouth. Serve it with 40 g (1½ oz) dried brown rice or noodles, cooked according to the packet instructions.

1 tablespoon plain flour
2 teaspoons Chinese five spice
450 g (1 lb) lean braising steak, visible fat
    removed, and cubed
low fat cooking spray
1 large red onion, sliced
2 red peppers, de-seeded and sliced
300 g (10½ oz) carrots, peeled and chopped
1 red chilli, de-seeded and sliced
10 cm (4 inch) fresh ginger, peeled and sliced
2 star anise
600 ml (20 fl oz) hot vegetable stock
2 heads pak choi, leaves divided

1 Mix together the flour and five spice in a shallow bowl. Add the steak and toss to coat. Spray a large lidded pan with the cooking spray and heat until hot. Add the steak and cook until browned. Add the onion, peppers, carrots, chilli, ginger and star anise and stir fry for 2–3 minutes just until everything is hot.
2 Stir in the stock, bring to the boil, then cover and reduce the heat to a gentle simmer. Cook for about 1 hour until the meat is tender, then stir in the pak choi. Leave it to wilt for a couple of minutes and then serve in shallow bowls.

Shredded pork with Mexican sauce

Calories per serving 265 **Serves 4**
15 mins prep + 10 mins resting, 1 hr 50 mins cooking
❄ **meat only**

This savoury sauce, enriched with dark chocolate, is truly amazing. If you cook the pork long and slow, it becomes incredibly tender.

550 g (1 lb 3 oz) boneless pork loin,
    visible fat removed
finely grated zest and juice of an orange
1 teaspoon cinnamon
½ teaspoon chilli flakes
2 teaspoons coriander seeds
1 teaspoon cumin seeds
1 teaspoon sesame seeds
3 black peppercorns
4 cloves
low fat cooking spray
1 onion, chopped
150 ml (5 fl oz) chicken stock
2 garlic cloves, crushed
1 teaspoon cocoa powder
400 g can chopped tomatoes
½ teaspoon cinnamon
30 g (1¼ oz) dark chocolate (minimum 70% cocoa
    solids), grated
salt and freshly ground black pepper

To serve
a handful of chopped fresh coriander, to garnish
a green salad of Little Gem leaves and cucumber

You will need a pestle and mortar or a rolling pin, for crushing; a lidded ovenproof dish

1 Preheat the oven to Gas Mark 7/220°C/fan oven 200°C. Put the pork in the lidded ovenproof dish. Mix the orange zest and juice together with the cinnamon and rub all over the pork. Season. Roast for 20 minutes, uncovered, then reduce the temperature to Gas Mark 3/160°C/fan oven 140°C. Cover and leave to cook for 1½ hours. Remove from the oven and leave to rest for 10 minutes.

2 For the sauce, roughly grind the chilli flakes, coriander, cumin and sesame seeds with the peppercorns and cloves in a mortar and pestle or place them all in a bowl and crush with the end of a rolling pin. Add them to a small non stick frying pan and dry fry for a minute or so until fragrant.

3 Meanwhile, spray a medium non stick frying pan with the cooking spray and heat until hot. Stir fry the onion for 5 minutes adding a little of the stock if it begins to stick. Add the garlic and cocoa and cook for another minute. Stir in the stock, tomatoes, spices from the other pan and the cinnamon. Reduce the heat and simmer gently for 10 minutes until thickened. Add the chocolate and stir until melted. Remove from the heat.

4 Slice the pork then shred using two forks to pull it apart. Serve it in a pile with the sauce and the salad on the side.

Try this The sauce can be served with other meats too. Enjoy it with a 125 g (4½ oz) cooked skinless, boneless chicken breast each.

Spanish pork pie

Calories per serving 304　　　　　**Serves 6**
40 mins prep, 50 mins cooking

This large and impressive pie is made with yeast pastry.
It's delicious with mixed vegetables such as broccoli and
runner beans or enjoy it cold in wedges for a picnic.

300 g (10½ oz) strong flour, 2 teaspoons reserved
a pinch of salt
1 tablespoon mixed dried herbs
1 teaspoon easy blend yeast from a sachet
1 egg white, beaten lightly

For the filling

1 tablespoon smoked paprika
300 g (10½ oz) lean pork fillet, visible fat
　　removed, and cubed
low fat cooking spray
1 onion, sliced thinly
2 red peppers, de-seeded and chopped
1 large carrot, peeled and grated
2 garlic cloves, crushed
450 g (1 lb) tomatoes, diced
25 g (1 oz) Parma ham (about 2 slices),
　　chopped
10 g (¼ oz) anchovy fillets in brine (about 2),
　　rinsed and chopped
100 ml (3½ fl oz) white wine

You will need a 20 cm (8 inch) springform tin

1　To make the pastry, place the flour in a large mixing
bowl and stir in the salt, herbs and yeast. Add 150 ml
(5 fl oz) hand hot water and stir to mix to a stiff dough.
Sprinkle a work surface with the reserved flour and knead
the dough for 5 minutes until smooth. Return to the bowl,
cover with a tea towel and leave in a warm place until
doubled in size (about 30 minutes).

2　Meanwhile, for the filling, sprinkle the paprika over
the pork and toss to mix. Spray a large, lidded non stick
frying pan with the cooking spray and heat until hot. Add
the pork and cook for about 3 minutes until browned and
sealed. Remove from the pan.

3　Spray the pan again with the cooking spray, add the
onion, peppers and carrot and cook over a medium to
low heat for 10 minutes adding a little water if they start
to stick. Return the pork to the pan with the remaining
ingredients letting the wine bubble up, then cover and
cook for 10 minutes. Most of the liquid should have
evaporated. Remove from the heat and cool slightly.

4　Preheat the oven to Gas Mark 4/180°C/fan oven 160°C.
Spray the springform tin with the cooking spray. Remove
the dough from the bowl and knead for a minute or so
to knock it back and redistribute the air. Cut off a third of
the dough for the lid then use the remainder to line the
springform tin. Using cool, wet hands and working quickly,
press the dough over the base and up the sides – you
might find it easier to roll it slightly first. Try to make the
sides an even height all around. Don't worry if it looks too
thin, it will rise on cooking. Spoon the pork mixture into the
tin. Fold the sides slightly over the filling.

5　Roll out the reserved dough to fit the pie. Brush the
rim with a little egg white, place the pastry lid on top and
pinch the edges together to seal. Pierce a couple of holes
in the top, brush all over with the egg white and bake for
40–50 minutes until golden. Let sit in the tin for a minute,
then release the springform and slide on to a plate or
board to serve.

cook's tip...

Easy blend yeast is the same as quick or fast
action yeast.

Lamb chops with bean salad

Calories per serving 332	Serves 4
Takes 20 mins + marinating	

finely grated zest and juice of a lemon
1 tablespoon chopped fresh rosemary
4 × 125 g (4½ oz) lamb chops, visible fat removed
low fat cooking spray
200 g (7 oz) fine green beans, trimmed and halved
200 g (7 oz) frozen peas

For the dressing
2 teaspoons extra virgin olive oil
1 teaspoon finely grated lemon zest and
     1 teaspoon juice
1 tablespoon chopped fresh mint
½ teaspoon runny honey
2 Little Gem lettuces, leaves separated

1 Mix together the lemon zest and juice and rosemary. Pour over the lamb, turning to coat on both sides. Set aside for at least 10 minutes or cover and chill overnight.

2 Heat a griddle pan until hot and spray the chops on both sides with the cooking spray. Griddle the lamb for a couple of minutes on each side. Alternatively, preheat the grill to medium and line the grill pan with foil. Cook the chops for about 10 minutes, turning occasionally.

3 Meanwhile, bring a pan of water to the boil, add the beans and peas and cook for 3–5 minutes until just tender. Drain well and return to the pan.

4 Mix the olive oil, lemon zest and juice, mint and honey together and pour over the beans and peas. Add the lettuce leaves and toss to coat. Serve a chop each on a bed of the salad.

Try this Make this with four 125 g (4½ oz) skinless, boneless chicken breasts, marinated and then pan fried in low fat cooking spray for 10–15 minutes, instead of the lamb chops.

Sage corn cakes

Calories per serving 107	Serves 4
Takes 20 mins	

Bake these the day before and then reheat in the oven for a quick and easy starter.

low fat cooking spray
4 × 22 g (¾ oz) turkey rashers
300 ml (10 fl oz) chicken or vegetable stock
75 g (2¾ oz) dried polenta
12 fresh sage leaves, chopped
2 fresh rosemary sprigs, leaves chopped
freshly ground black pepper

To serve
150 g (5½ oz) mixed leaves
2 tablespoons balsamic vinegar

You will need a muffin tray

1 Preheat the oven to Gas Mark 6/200°C/fan oven 180°C. Spray four of the holes in the muffin tray with the cooking spray and line the four holes with one turkey rasher each.

2 Place the stock in a small non stick pan and bring to the boil. Add the polenta and cook, stirring continuously for 1–2 minutes until thick. Stir in the herbs and some black pepper.

3 Spoon the polenta into the lined holes and bake for 10 minutes until golden on top. Serve a cake each, with some leaves, dressed with the balsamic vinegar.

Lamb tagine

Calories per serving 413

Serves 4

15 mins prep, 1 hr cooking

❄ **stew only**

A richly flavoured Moroccan stew.

2 teaspoons ground ginger

2 teaspoons ground coriander

1 teaspoon turmeric

½ teaspoon cayenne or chilli powder

1 teaspoon cinnamon

450 g (1 lb) lean lamb steaks, visible
    fat removed, and cubed

low fat cooking spray

1 onion or red onion, sliced

2 garlic cloves, crushed

400 g carton passata

150 ml (5 fl oz) lamb or chicken stock

60 g (2 oz) raisins

For the couscous

1 lemon

1 courgette, cut into chunks

1 red pepper, de-seeded and cut into chunks

1 yellow pepper, de-seeded and cut into chunks

1 tablespoon coriander seeds, crushed roughly

150 g (5½ oz) dried couscous

200 ml (7 fl oz) boiling water

You will need a lidded flameproof and ovenproof pan

1 Preheat the oven to Gas Mark 5/190°C/fan oven 170°C. Mix together the spices on a shallow plate, add the lamb and toss to coat. Spray the pan with the cooking spray and heat until hot. Add the lamb and brown for 3–5 minutes. Add the remaining tagine ingredients, bring to the boil, cover and transfer to the oven. Cook for 1 hour.

2 For the couscous, finely grate the zest from the lemon and set aside. Quarter the lemon and place in a shallow roasting tin with the courgette and peppers. Scatter over the coriander seeds and spray with the cooking spray. Roast for 30–40 minutes, turning occasionally until lightly charred.

3 Meanwhile, put the couscous in a bowl and pour over the boiling water, cover with cling film and leave to soak for 10 minutes. Fluff with a fork and stir into the roasted vegetables for the final 5 minutes cooking time.

4 Just before serving, stir the lemon zest into the tagine. Serve with a quarter of the vegetable couscous each.

Creamy leek pies

Calories per serving 330　　　Serves 4

30 mins prep, 15 mins cooking

60 g (2 oz) low fat spread

400 g (14 oz) leeks, sliced thinly

25 g (½ oz) flour

700 ml (1¼ pints) skimmed milk

4 teaspoons wholegrain mustard

4 × 45 g (1½ oz) sheets filo pastry, measuring
　　50 × 24 cm (20 × 9½ inches), defrosted if frozen

low fat cooking spray

You will need four gratin dishes, at least
14 cm (5½ inches) wide and about 3 cm (1¼ inch) deep

1　Preheat the oven to Gas Mark 6/200°C/fan oven 180°C.

2　Melt half the spread in a large non stick pan and when
sizzling, add the leeks. Cook, stirring occasionally for
5–10 minutes until soft. In a bowl, mix the remaining
spread with the flour to form a paste. Add the paste to
the leeks and cook, stirring, until it has melted. Cook,
stirring for a minute.

3　Remove from the heat and adding the milk a little at a
time, mix into the leeks stirring until the mixture is smooth
before adding more. Return the pan to the heat, bring to
the boil and cook, stirring continuously until thickened.
Remove from the heat and stir in the mustard.

4　Spoon the mixture into the four gratin dishes. Spray
each sheet of filo with the cooking spray and scrunch a
sheet on top of each dish. Spray the top again. Bake for
10–15 minutes until golden.

Try this For a meaty version, stir in a total of 60 g (2 oz)
shredded wafer thin ham.

Five spice duck in lettuce

Calories per serving 156　　　Serves 4

15 mins prep, 30 mins cooking

Serving this stir fry in lettuce leaves looks lovely but you
could also serve it with 40 g (1½ oz) dried brown rice each,
cooked according to the packet instructions.

low fat cooking spray

350 g (12 oz) skinless, boneless duck breast

2 celery sticks, sliced finely

1 carrot, peeled and cut into very thin sticks

2 teaspoons finely chopped fresh ginger

250 g (9 oz) mushrooms, chopped

2 teaspoons Chinese five spice

2 garlic cloves, chopped

200 g bag beansprouts

3 light tablespoons soy sauce, plus extra to serve

4 Iceberg lettuce leaves

1　Preheat the oven to Gas Mark 5/190°C/fan oven 170°C.
Spray a small roasting tin with the cooking spray, add the
duck and roast for 20–30 minutes until brown and firm
to touch. Remove from the oven and cool slightly before
dicing.

2　Spray a wok or large non stick frying pan with the
cooking spray and heat until hot. Add the celery, carrot
and ginger and stir fry for 2 minutes. Add the mushrooms,
Chinese five spice and garlic and continue cooking for
another 2 minutes.

3　Add the beansprouts with the duck and cook for a
minute before adding the soy sauce. Stir to combine and
ensure everything is hot before serving in the lettuce
leaves.

Peppered steak with chips

Calories per serving 456	Serves 2
10 mins prep, 30 mins cooking	

low fat cooking spray
550 g (1 lb 3 oz) potatoes, peeled and cut
    into long and chunky chips
2 tablespoons mixed peppercorns, crushed lightly
salt
2 × 150 g (5½ oz) rump steaks, visible fat removed
80 g (3 oz) long stem broccoli
2 tablespoons wholegrain or Dijon mustard

1 Preheat the oven to Gas Mark 7/220°C/fan oven 200°C. Spray a non stick baking sheet with the cooking spray.
2 Bring a large pan of water to the boil, add the potatoes, bring back to the boil and simmer for 3 minutes. Drain and dry thoroughly in a kitchen towel. Place on the baking sheet and spray generously with the cooking spray, turning to coat each chip. Bake for 25–30 minutes, turning occasionally until golden and cooked through.
3 Meanwhile, mix the peppercorns with a little salt and press into both sides of the steaks. Spray a non stick frying pan with the cooking spray. Heat until hot then cook the steaks over a high heat, as desired (see Cook's tip). Remove from the pan, cover with foil and leave for about 3 minutes.
4 Bring a small pan of water to the boil, add the broccoli and cook for 3–4 minutes until just tender. Drain.
5 Serve the steaks with the chips, broccoli and 1 tablespoon of mustard each.

cook's tip...

For rare, cook the steak over a high heat for 1 minute on each side; for medium, 2 minutes on each side; and for well done, 3 minutes on each side.

Monkfish with Parma ham

Calories per serving 293	Serves 2
10 mins prep, 20 mins cooking	

Quick and easy, this is an impressive dinner for two.

2 Parma ham slices
2 thin lemon slices
2 × 110 g (4 oz) monkfish tails
125 g (4½ oz) cherry tomatoes (optional)
low fat cooking spray
450 g (1 lb) potatoes, peeled and chopped
140 g (5 oz) green beans, trimmed
salt and freshly ground black pepper

1 Preheat the oven to Gas Mark 6/200°C/fan oven 180°C. Lay the Parma ham slices on a board, top each with a lemon slice and then the monkfish. Wrap up and place in a shallow ovenproof dish with the tomatoes, if using. Spray everything with the cooking spray and bake for 15–20 minutes until the fish is cooked through.
2 Meanwhile, bring a lidded pan of water to the boil and add the potatoes. Cover and simmer for 10–15 minutes until tender. Drain and mash then season.
3 At the same time, bring a small pan of water to the boil, add the beans and cook for 3–4 minutes until just tender. Drain.
4 Serve a pile of mash with a piece of fish each. Spoon over any juices and serve the green beans and tomatoes, if using, on the side.

Try this Monkfish is lovely for a special occasion but quite expensive. Make it an everyday dish by using the same amount of pollack or haddock.

Salmon puffs

Calories per serving 267	Serves 4
Takes 45 mins	

Individual dishes of baked choux pastry puff up beautifully around a creamy mixture of smoked salmon, asparagus and fresh dill.

low fat cooking spray

For the choux pastry
60 g (2 oz) plain flour
40 g (1½ oz) low fat spread
a pinch of salt
2 eggs, beaten

For the filling
450 ml (16 fl oz) skimmed milk
200 g (7 oz) fine asparagus, chopped
25 g (1 oz) cornflour
125 g (4½ oz) smoked salmon, shredded
     into thin strips
2 teaspoons fresh dill or ½ teaspoon dried
freshly ground black pepper

You will need four ovenproof gratin dishes; a piping bag, if using

1 Preheat the oven to Gas Mark 6/200°C/fan oven 180°C. Spray the gratin dishes with the cooking spray.
2 To make the choux pastry, sift the flour on to a plate and set aside. Put the low fat spread and 150 ml (5 fl oz) water into a medium sized pan. Bring to the boil, remove from the heat and quickly add the flour to the mixture, stirring continuously. Once the mixture has come together smoothly, set aside to cool for a few minutes.
3 Stir the salt into the choux mixture and add a little of the beaten eggs, beating to combine before adding more. Continue to add the eggs, beating really hard to incorporate air (air is the only raising agent in choux pastry) until all of has been added.

4 Use a teaspoon to dollop the mixture around the edges of the gratin dishes to create a container for the filling; you might find it easier to use a piping bag. Bake for 20 minutes until puffed up and golden.
5 Meanwhile, make the filling. Place the milk and asparagus in a large pan, bring to the boil and gently simmer for 5 minutes until the asparagus is just tender. Mix the cornflour with a tablespoon or two of cold water, add a little hot milk and mix. Pour the mixture back into the pan and bring up to the boil. Stir for 1 or 2 minutes until thickened. Stir in the smoked salmon and dill and some black pepper; it should be salty enough, thanks to the salmon. Remove the dishes from the oven and spoon the salmon mixture into the middle, bake for 5–10 minutes until piping hot. Serve in the dishes.

chocolate
(heaven)

Are you a chocolate lover? Then you'll love the incredible chocolate recipes in this chapter. You'll enjoy every delicious spoonful of the Hot Chocolate Prune Pud or you might fancy a Chocolate Truffle or two. And if you can convince yourself to share the Marbled Chocolate Cheesecake with friends, everyone will be raving about it.

Black Forest gâteau on page 156

Black Forest gâteau

Calories per serving 200	**Serves 10**
20 mins prep, 35 mins cooking + 30 mins cooling	

 sponge only

For the cake

75 g (2¾ oz) low fat spread

110 g (4 oz) caster sugar

140 g (5 oz) plain flour

40 g (1½ oz) cocoa powder, ½ teaspoon reserved

1 teaspoon baking powder

1 teaspoon bicarbonate of soda

2 eggs

150 ml (5 fl oz) skimmed milk

For the filling

300 g (10½ oz) 0% fat Greek yogurt

1 teaspoon vanilla extract

30 g (1¼ oz) icing sugar, sifted

425 g can cherries in natural juice, drained,
  reserving 4 tablespoons juice

You will need two 23 cm (9 inch) baking tins;
non stick baking parchment

1 Preheat the oven to Gas Mark 6/200°C/fan oven 180°C.
Line the base of the tins with the baking parchment.

2 To make the cake, place all the ingredients in a food
processor and blend until smooth. Alternatively, use an
electric whisk to soften the spread in a large mixing bowl.
Add the other ingredients and beat well.

3 Pour the mixture into the tins. Cook for 25–35 minutes
until springy to touch. Remove from the oven, invert on to
a wire rack and remove the paper base. Leave to cool for
about 30 minutes.

4 To make the filling, beat together the yogurt, vanilla
and icing sugar until smooth. Place one cake on a serving
plate. Drizzle over the reserved cherry juice and then
spread over the yogurt mixture. Scatter over the cherries
and place the second cake on top. Dust with the reserved
cocoa and slice to serve.

Chocolate lime meringue pots

Calories per serving 179	**Serves 2**
Takes 15 mins + 4 hrs chilling	

low fat cooking spray

1 egg white

50 g (1¾ oz) caster sugar

finely grated zest of ½ a lime

20 g (¾ oz) dark chocolate (minimum 70% cocoa solids)

½ teaspoon icing sugar

2 teaspoons 0% fat Greek yogurt

50 g (1¾ oz) blueberries, to serve

You will need two small pudding basins or ramekins;
a heatproof bowl

1 Spray the pudding basins with the cooking spray. With
an electric whisk, whisk the egg white in a clean, grease-
free bowl until it holds stiff peaks. Whisk in half of the sugar
until it is thick and glossy.

2 Place the remainder of the sugar in a small pan with a
tablespoon of water and bring slowly to the boil, swirling
to dissolve. Once all the sugar has dissolved, boil for
1 minute and stir in the lime zest to make a syrup.

3 With the whisk running, pour the syrup into the whites
in a steady stream and continue whisking until well
combined. Divide the meringue between the basins or
ramekins, level the surface and chill for 3–4 hours.

4 When ready to serve, place the chocolate in a heatproof
bowl over a pan of simmering water for 2–3 minutes until
melted. Remove from the heat.

5 Make the sauce. Stir the icing sugar into the chocolate
and then stir in the yogurt with 1 tablespoon of warm
water. Mix well until smooth and glossy.

6 Run a knife round the basins and tip the meringue out
on to serving plates. They won't be completely smooth
but will hold their shape. Drizzle over the chocolate sauce.
Serve immediately with the blueberries on the side.

Classic choc chip muffins

Calories per serving 138   **Makes 12**
10 mins prep, 20 mins cooking

This is a lighter version of the classic recipe but just as delicious.

200 g (7 oz) plain flour
2 teaspoons baking powder
75 g (2¾ oz) caster sugar
a pinch of salt
1 egg, beaten
200 ml (7 fl oz) skimmed milk
25 g (1 oz) low fat spread, melted
½ teaspoon vanilla extract
40 g (1½ oz) dark chocolate chips
40 g (1½ oz) white chocolate chips

You will need a 12 hole muffin tin; 12 muffin cases

1 Preheat the oven to Gas Mark 6/200°C/fan oven 180°C. Line the muffin tin with the muffin cases. Sift the flour and baking powder into a large bowl and stir in the sugar and salt.

2 In a separate bowl, beat together the egg, milk, low fat spread and vanilla. Add the egg mixture to the flour with the chocolate chips and stir together quickly. Do not over stir; it is better to have a slightly lumpy texture. Spoon into the muffin cases and bake for 15–20 minutes until golden and risen. Cool on a wire rack.

Ice cream balls

Calories per serving 177   **Serves 6**
Takes 20 mins + 1 hr freezing

360 g (12 oz) low fat vanilla flavoured ice cream
120 g (4½ oz) dark chocolate (minimum 70% cocoa solids) or milk chocolate
finely grated zest of 1 orange
2 tablespoons silver balls, to decorate

You will need a baking tray that fits in the freezer; non stick baking parchment; a heatproof bowl

1 Line the baking tray with the baking parchment. Remove the ice cream from the freezer, take the lid off and leave to soften for a few minutes at room temperature. If you have a superfreeze button on your freezer, switch it on.

2 Using a tablespoon, scoop 18 small balls on to the tray; they should weigh 20 g (¾ oz) each. Poke a cocktail stick into each and freeze for at least 1 hour.

3 Place the chocolate in a heatproof bowl over a pan of simmering water for 2–3 minutes, until just melted. Remove from the heat. Stir the orange zest into the chocolate.

4 Take hold of the cocktail stick and lift each ice cream ball off the tray. Use a small spoon to drizzle the chocolate over the ice cream. Return to the tray and sprinkle over the silver balls to decorate. The chocolate will set almost immediately, so you have to work quite quickly to get the balls to stick.

5 Serve three ice cream balls per person immediately. Alternatively, return to the freezer and use as desired.

V Try this Additional flavours can be added to the ice cream. You might try the finely grated zest of 1 lemon or lime , ¼ teaspoon of cinnamon or, if you like it spicy, a pinch of chilli powder stirred into the chocolate.

Marbled chocolate cheesecake

Calories per serving 181   **Serves 8**
Takes 20 mins + 2 hrs chilling

Sheet gelatine is much easier to use than powdered and most supermarkets now stock it in the home baking section. Serve with 60 g (2 oz) raspberries per person.

8 g (¼ oz) gelatine sheets (4 sheets)
110 g (4 oz) reduced fat oaty biscuits, crushed
40 g (1½ oz) low fat spread, melted
40 g (1½ oz) dark chocolate (minimum 70% cocoa solids)
150 g (5½ oz) reduced fat custard
250 g (9 oz) extra light low fat soft cheese
25 g (1 oz) caster sugar
1 teaspoon vanilla extract
2 egg whites

You will need a 20 cm (8 inch) springform baking tin; non stick baking parchment; a heatproof bowl

1 Soak the gelatine in cold water for 5 minutes. Line the base of the springform tin with the baking parchment.
2 Combine the biscuits and melted low fat spread and press down firmly into the base of the prepared tin. Chill until required.
3 Put the chocolate in a heatproof bowl over a pan of simmering water for 2–3 minutes until melted. Remove from the heat.
4 In a bowl, beat together the custard, soft cheese, sugar and vanilla.
5 In a clean grease-free bowl, whisk the egg whites until they hold soft peaks. Carefully fold into the custard mix.

6 Drain the gelatine and squeeze out any excess water. Place in a large pan and heat gently until dissolved. Remove from the heat and stir the custard mix into the gelatine. Pour the custard mixture over the biscuit base and level the surface. Drizzle over the chocolate and swirl with a fine skewer to marble the top. Chill for 2 hours before serving.

cook's tip...

Ring the changes and stir the finely grated zest of an orange into the chocolate mixture for added flavour.

Impress your friends with a delicious slice
of this stunning chocolate cheesecake.

Chocolate éclairs

60 g (2 oz) plain flour

50 g (1¾ oz) low fat spread

2 eggs, beaten

250 g tub Quark

2 tablespoons icing sugar

½ teaspoon vanilla extract

40 g (1½ oz) icing sugar

15 g (½ oz) cocoa powder

You will need non stick baking parchment; a piping bag with a wide nozzle

1 Preheat the oven to Gas Mark 6/200°C/fan oven 180°C. Line a baking sheet with the baking parchment.

2 Sift the flour into a bowl. Put the low fat spread in a heavy based medium sized pan with 150 ml (5 fl oz) water. Heat gently until the spread has melted, then bring to the boil. Take off the heat, quickly adding all the flour. Beat rapidly with a wooden spoon until smooth. Leave to cool.

3 Add a little egg and beat until combined. Continue, adding the egg until you have a thick paste that holds its shape. Beat vigorously to incorporate as much air as possible. Transfer to the piping bag.

4 Pipe twelve 8 cm (3¼ inch) lines on to the baking sheet and bake for 15–20 minutes until puffed up. Remove from the oven and immediately pierce a small hole in the side to release the steam. Set aside to cool on a wire rack.

5 Beat together the Quark, icing sugar and vanilla until smooth. Carefully slit the sides of the éclairs and fill with the Quark mixture using a spoon or piping bag.

6 Sift the icing sugar and cocoa into a small bowl and add 2 tablespoons of water a little at a time until you have a thick glacé icing. Spoon over the tops of the éclairs and leave to set before serving. Once filled, eat within an hour.

Chocolate orange mousse

This intense chocolate mousse with a hint of orange liqueur is definitely a special occasion dessert.

30 g (1¼ oz) dark chocolate (minimum 70% cocoa solids), broken

30 g (1¼ oz) light condensed milk

4 sponge fingers (22 g/¾ oz in total)

2 teaspoons orange flavoured liqueur

1 egg white

You will need a small heatproof bowl

1 Place the chocolate in small heatproof bowl over a pan of gently simmering water. Leave to melt for about 5 minutes, remove from the heat and stir in the condensed milk.

2 Meanwhile, break the sponge fingers into four pieces each and place in a small bowl. Drizzle over the liqueur, stir to mix and spoon into the bottom of two small serving glasses.

3 Whisk the egg white until it holds soft peaks then carefully fold into the chocolate mixture – you might find it easier to add a little of the white, beat that in to loosen the mixture and then carefully fold in the rest. Spoon on top of the fingers and chill for an hour before serving.

cook's tip...

Brandy or rum work just as well as orange flavoured liqueur.

Chocolate flapjacks

Calories per serving 112   **Makes 12**

5 mins prep, 20 mins cooking + 30 mins cooling

low fat cooking spray
60 g (2 oz) low fat spread
50 g (1¾ oz) light brown sugar
2 tablespoons golden syrup
finely grated zest of 1 orange
175 g (6 oz) porridge oats
25 g (1 oz) milk chocolate

You will need an 18 cm (7 inch) square baking tin;
a heatproof bowl

1 Preheat the oven to Gas Mark 4/180°C/fan oven 160°C.
Spray the baking tin with the cooking spray.

2 Place the low fat spread, sugar and syrup in a large pan
and melt over a gentle heat. Remove from the heat and stir
in the orange zest and oats. Spoon into the baking tin and
level the surface. Bake for 15–20 minutes.

3 Meanwhile, place the chocolate in a heatproof bowl
over a pan of simmering water for 2–3 minutes until
melted. Remove from the heat.

4 Remove the baking tin from the oven and cool for
5 minutes. Cut the flapjack into 12 rectangles and drizzle
over the chocolate. Leave to cool in the tin for about 30
minutes. They will keep in an airtight container for 3 days.

Pear and chocolate pudding

Calories per serving 147   **Serves 6**

10 mins prep, 30 mins cooking

This pudding is sure to become a favourite. For added
indulgence, mix 1 tablespoon of icing sugar into a
150 g pot of 0% fat Greek yogurt with ½ teaspoon of
vanilla extract and serve 25 g (1 oz) each.

low fat cooking spray
2 pears (about 340 g/12 oz in total), peeled,
    cored and sliced
1 tablespoon golden syrup
3 eggs
75 g (2¾ oz) caster sugar
50 g (1¾ oz) cocoa powder

You will need a 1.5 litre (2¾ pint) shallow ovenproof dish

1 Preheat the oven to Gas Mark 4/180°C/fan oven 160°C.
Spray the ovenproof dish with the cooking spray.

2 Arrange the pears in the base of the dish and drizzle
over the syrup.

3 Place the eggs and caster sugar in a large bowl and
whisk until thick and creamy; the whisks should leave a
trail when lifted. Sift over the cocoa powder and carefully
fold in. Spoon the mixture on top of the pears and bake
for 25–30 minutes until springy to the touch. Serve warm.

Baked chocolate custards

Calories per serving 177 Serves 2
10 mins prep + 5 mins cooling, 40 mins cooking

Serve these warm for a creamy, comforting treat or chill to bring out the chocolate flavour even more.

250 ml (9 fl oz) skimmed milk
1 tablespoon soft brown sugar
15 g (½ oz) cocoa powder, reserving ½ teaspoon, for dusting
½ teaspoon vanilla extract
2 eggs, beaten
a kettleful of boiling water

You will need two ramekins; a shallow roasting tin

1 Preheat the oven to Gas Mark 3/160°C/fan oven 140°C.
2 Place the milk and sugar in a pan and bring to the boil, stirring to dissolve the sugar. Remove from the heat and whisk in the cocoa, then leave to cool for about 5 minutes.
3 Stir in the vanilla and the eggs. Place the ramekins in a shallow roasting tin. Pour the milk mixture into the ramekins through a strainer to remove the eggy threads. Pour boiling water into the roasting tin to come halfway up the ramekins.
4 Bake for 30–40 minutes until just set but with a slight wobble. Remove from the oven and leave to cool slightly. Serve warm or leave to go cold and then chill.

Hot chocolate prune puds

Calories per serving 163 Serves 4
15 mins prep, 15 mins cooking

low fat cooking spray
210 g can prunes in natural juice (remove stones if necessary)
75 ml (3 fl oz) skimmed milk
½ teaspoon vanilla extract
30 g (1¼ oz) plain flour, sifted
25 g (1 oz) light brown sugar
40 g (1½ oz) dark chocolate (minimum 70% cocoa solids), broken into pieces
2 egg whites
2 teaspoons cocoa powder, sifted, reserving ½ teaspoon, for dusting

You will need four ramekins or small pudding basins; a heatproof bowl

1 Preheat the oven to Gas Mark 6/200°C/fan oven 180°C. Spray the pudding basins with the cooking spray.
2 Place the prunes and their juice in a mixing bowl with the milk, vanilla, flour and sugar. Blend with a hand held blender or transfer to a liquidiser and blend until smooth.
3 Meanwhile, place the chocolate in a heatproof bowl over a pan of simmering water for 2–3 minutes until melted. Remove from the heat.
4 Whisk the egg whites in a clean grease-free bowl until stiff. Stir the chocolate and cocoa into the prune mixture. Add a spoonful of the whites to the chocolate mixture to slacken it then carefully fold in the remaining mixture. Spoon into the ramekins or basins and bake for 15 minutes until risen and set on the top. Dust with the reserved cocoa and serve in the ramekins.

These rich chocolate puds have a lovely soufflé texture.

Chocolate truffles

Calories per serving 47　　　　　　**Makes 10**
Takes 15 mins + 15 mins setting

V Try this Various flavours can be added along with the condensed milk: try ½ teaspoon of finely grated orange zest or ½ teaspoon almond essence. Roll the truffles in ½ teaspoon cocoa instead of the sugar strands.

What better way to end a meal? Or you can take a box to a friend as a present.

25 g (1 oz) sponge fingers, broken
60 g (2 oz) dark chocolate (minimum 70% cocoa
　　solids) or milk chocolate, broken into squares
40 g (1½ oz) light condensed milk,
　　at room temperature
5 g (¼ oz) chocolate sugar strands

You will need a heatproof bowl; small paper cases

1 Place the broken sponge fingers in a bowl and use the end of a rolling pin to make them into crumbs. Set aside.
2 Place the chocolate in a heatproof bowl over a pan of gently simmering water and leave to melt for about 5 minutes. Remove from the heat and stir in the condensed milk and sponge finger crumbs. Mix well.
3 Rinse your hands under cold water and dry them before rolling the balls. (This will keep your hands cool and prevent the chocolate from melting.)
4 Working quickly, take walnut size pieces, roll each of them into a ball and then press the chocolate sugar strands into the top of each one. Place in small paper cases and leave to set for 15 minutes before serving.

puds + bakes

Make yourself something fabulous today. There's lots of variety here – how about a retro classic such as the Baked Alaskas or a new version of an old favourite, such as the Strawberry Trifle Loaf? Be sure to try the Coconut Castles with Mango Salsa too – not only are they quick to make but the flavour is gorgeous. And for a special occasion, a slice of Frozen Strawberry Meringue Torte really hits the spot.

Strawberry trifle loaf on page 172

Strawberry trifle loaf

Calories per serving 89 Serves 6
Takes 15 mins + 2 hrs setting

This easy pudding is impressive enough to serve at a supper party but equally good for a family treat.

low fat cooking spray
80 g (3 oz) sponge fingers (about 14)
350 g (12 oz) strawberries, hulled
11 g sachet sugar free strawberry jelly
100 ml (3½ fl oz) boiling water
150 g pot 0% fat Greek yogurt

You will need a 900 g (2 lb) loaf tin

1 Spray the loaf tin with the cooking spray and then line it with cling film, pressing and smoothing it into the corners.
2 Arrange half of the sponge fingers along the bottom of the tin, breaking them if necessary to fit, but remembering that this will be the top so it should be quite neat.
3 Roughly chop half of the strawberries and place them in a liquidiser, or use a hand held blender, and whizz until smooth.
4 To make up the jelly, sprinkle the sachet over the boiling water and stir to dissolve. Add the strawberry purée and yogurt and mix well. Spoon enough over the sponge fingers in the tin to just cover. Chill for 5 minutes until just set. Make the remaining mixture up to 500 ml (18 fl oz). Arrange the sliced strawberries on top of the set mixture, then carefully pour over the remaining jelly. Tap to level then top with the remaining fingers. Chill for 2 hours until firm.
5 To serve, invert a long serving plate over the top of the tin, turn it over and tip out the trifle. Carefully remove the cling film. Decorate with the reserved strawberries and serve in slices.

Baked Alaskas

Calories per serving 207 Serves 2
Takes 15 mins

Fancy something retro? Try these lovely puddings.

1 egg white
25 g (1 oz) golden caster sugar
2 × 30 g (1¼ oz) trifle sponges
1 tablespoon reduced sugar raspberry jam
50 g (1¾ oz) reduced fat vanilla ice cream

1 Preheat the grill to medium. Whisk the egg white in a clean, grease-free bowl until it holds stiff peaks. Add the sugar a little at a time, whisking between additions until it is really stiff and glossy.
2 Place the trifle sponges on a baking tray. Spread the jam over the top of each and add a 25 g (1 oz) scoop of ice cream. Spread the meringue over the ice cream so it totally covers and seals it in – you could pipe it for extra effect.
3 Place under the grill for 1–3 minutes until golden, watching it carefully as it can catch. Serve immediately.

V Try this Weight Watchers reduced sugar raspberry jam would work well.

Steamed lemon pudding

Calories per serving 263
30 mins prep, 1½ hrs cooking

Serves 6

low fat cooking spray
110 g (4 oz) golden caster sugar
2 lemons, 1 sliced thinly
60 g (2 oz) low fat spread
2 eggs, beaten
150 g (5½ oz) self raising flour, sifted
½ a kettleful of boiling water
60 g (2 oz) light brown sugar

You will need an 850 ml (1½ pint) pudding basin; a piece of non stick baking parchment cut to double the diameter of the basin, with a fold in the middle; some string

1 Spray the pudding basin with the cooking spray. Sprinkle 2 teaspoons of the caster sugar into the pudding basin and tap around to coat. Place the sliced lemon in the base of the pudding basin and around the edges.

2 Place the remaining caster sugar and low fat spread in a large mixing bowl and beat until pale and smooth. Gradually add the eggs, beating between additions. Finely grate the zest from the other lemon and fold it into the egg mixture along with the flour.

3 Spoon the mixture into the basin, and put the baking parchment over the top. Tie the string around the basin securely to keep it in place. Place the basin in a steamer or put an upturned saucer in the bottom of a large lidded pan and sit the basin on it instead. Carefully pour boiling water into the steamer or pan, about halfway up the basin. Cover the pan with a lid and steam the pudding for 1½ hours.

4 To make the syrup, squeeze the juice from the zested lemon into a small heavy based pan, add the brown sugar and heat until dissolved. Bring to the boil and continue simmering for about 5 minutes until you have a syrup. Carefully remove the pudding from the pan and turn out on to a plate. Serve in wedges, with syrup poured over.

Poached pears and butterscotch

Calories per serving 193
Takes 25 mins

Serves 2

These lightly poached pears take on a hint of lemon which cuts through the richness of the butterscotch sauce.

2 pears
2 teaspoons sugar
2 lemon zest strips, pith removed

For the sauce
25 g (1 oz) low fat spread
25 g (1 oz) soft brown sugar
15 g (½ oz) low fat soft cheese

You will need a corer or small sharp knife

1 Peel the pears, leaving the stalk in place, and cut a thin slice from the bottom so that they stand upright. Bore into the base with a corer or a small, sharp knife and remove the core, to about three-quarters of the way up.

2 Place the sugar in a small lidded pan, big enough to hold both pears with 200 ml (7 fl oz) water and the lemon zest. Bring to the boil and stir to dissolve the sugar. Add the pears, cover and simmer gently for 10 minutes or until soft (this will depend on the ripeness of the pears). Remove from the heat.

3 In another pan, melt the low fat spread with the brown sugar and let it boil for 1 minute. Remove from the heat and whisk in the soft cheese.

4 Drain the pears, discarding the juice and serve a pear each, with the sauce drizzled over.

Raspberry meringues

Calories per serving 103   Makes 8

15 mins prep, 1 hr cooking + 1 hr cooling

Everyone will love these pretty meringues.

2 egg whites

110 g (4 oz) caster sugar

25 g (1 oz) ground almonds

110 g (4 oz) raspberries

150 g (5½ oz) virtually fat free fromage frais

2 tablespoons icing sugar

a couple of drops of red or pink food colouring
(optional)

You will need two baking sheets; non stick baking parchment

1   Preheat the oven to Gas Mark 1/140°C/fan oven 120°C. Line the two baking sheets with the baking parchment.

2   Whisk the egg whites in a clean, grease-free bowl until they hold stiff peaks. Add half of the caster sugar and whisk until glossy. Mix together the remaining caster sugar and almonds then fold into the meringue with the raspberries.

3   Place heaped dessertspoonfuls of the meringue on to the trays to make 16 meringues. Bake for 1 hour until firm (if they aren't, keep the oven on for another 15 minutes), switch the oven off and leave for a further 30 minutes to dry out. Remove from the oven and allow to cool completely for about one hour.

4   Mix the fromage frais and icing sugar together with the food colouring, if using. To serve, place two meringues in each of eight bowls and drizzle over the fromage frais mixture. Repeat with all the meringues.

Ⓥ Try this Omit the fromage frais and icing sugar and crumble the meringues into 400 g (14 oz) of low fat fruity yogurt for a deliciously low fat Eton Mess.

The meringues can be kept for a day or so in an airtight container – any longer and the raspberries will start to soften them.

Coconut castles with mango salsa

Calories per serving 194
15 mins prep, 15 mins cooking
 Serves 4

low fat cooking spray
10 g (¼ oz) desiccated coconut
50 g (1¾ oz) caster sugar
2 eggs
75 g (2¾ oz) self raising flour
finely grated zest and juice of 2 limes
1 mango, peeled, stoned and diced

You will need four ovenproof pudding basins or ramekins

1 Preheat the oven to Gas Mark 4/180°C/fan oven 160°C. Spray the pudding basins or ramekins with the cooking spray. Divide the coconut between the pudding basins or ramekins.
2 Place the sugar and eggs in a large bowl and using an electric whisk, whisk until thick and creamy. Sift over the flour and carefully fold in with the lime zest. Spoon into the basins and bake for 10–15 minutes until golden and springy to touch.
3 Meanwhile, place half the mango and the lime juice in a food processor or blender and blend until smooth. Stir in the remaining mango and set aside.
4 To serve, loosen the puddings with a round-ended knife. Tip out on to a serving plate and top with the mango sauce.

Fruits of the forest sponge

Calories per serving 247
20 mins prep, 40 mins cooking
  Serves 6

low fat cooking spray
380 g pack frozen fruits of the forest
110 g (4 oz) brown sugar
75 g (2¾ oz) low fat spread
2 eggs, beaten
125 g (4½ oz) self raising flour
1 teaspoon mixed spice

You will need a 22 cm (8½ inch) round ovenproof dish

1 Preheat the oven to Gas Mark 4/180°C/fan oven 160°C. Spray the ovenproof dish with the cooking spray. Place the fruits in a pan, add 2 tablespoons of the brown sugar and gently simmer for 5 minutes until the juices are beginning to run. Using a slotted spoon, place the fruit in the bottom of the dish, leaving the juices in the pan.
2 Place the remaining sugar in a mixing bowl with the low fat spread and beat until pale and creamy. Add the eggs a little at a time, whisking between additions. Sift over the flour and spice and gently fold in. Spoon the sponge mixture over the fruits and bake for 30–40 minutes until the sponge springs back.
3 Heat the pan of juices over a medium heat until hot and syrupy. Turn the pudding out on to a serving plate and serve with the syrup poured over.

cook's tip...

Keep a pack of frozen fruits handy in the freezer and try this with a summer fruits mix for a change.

Frozen strawberry meringue torte

Calories per serving 170 **Serves 8**
Takes 15 mins + 3 hrs freezing + 20 mins standing

Frozen meringue takes on a lovely creamy flavour with a mousse-like texture.

low fat cooking spray
150 g (5½ oz) amaretti biscuits, crushed
50 g (1¾ oz) low fat spread, melted
2 egg whites
60 g (2 oz) caster sugar
250 g (9 oz) ripe strawberries, hulled and
    chopped finely
1 tablespoon lemon juice
1 teaspoon vanilla extract

For the coulis
200 g (7 oz) strawberries, hulled and chopped
1 tablespoon icing sugar

You will need a 23 cm (9 inch) springform baking tin; non stick baking parchment

1 Line the base of the baking tin with baking parchment and spray the sides with the cooking spray.
2 Mix together the biscuits and low fat spread in a bowl and press into the base of the tin. Chill until required.
3 Place the egg whites in a clean, grease-free bowl and whisk until they hold stiff peaks. Add the sugar a tablespoon at a time, whisking to combine between additions. Fold in the strawberries, lemon juice and vanilla. Spoon on top of the biscuit base, level the surface and freeze for at least 3 hours.
4 To make the coulis, blitz the strawberries and sugar in a liquidiser, or use a hand held blender, and then push through a sieve.

5 To serve, remove the torte from the freezer, leave to stand for 20 minutes and then slice. Serve with the coulis drizzled over.

If you make purées often, it's worth investing in a nylon sieve. A metal one can slightly discolour the fruit and sometimes creates a slightly metallic taste.

This strawberry meringue torte is simply divine and tastes as good as it looks.

Gingered banana bake

Calories per serving 242   Serves 6
10 mins prep, 40 mins cooking

This rich and warming pudding forms its own scrumptious sauce underneath.

low fat cooking spray
150 g (5½ oz) self raising flour
1 teaspoon ground ginger
150 g (5½ oz) brown sugar
1 banana, mashed
175 ml (6 fl oz) skimmed milk
40 g (1½ oz) low fat spread, melted
20 g (¾ oz) stem ginger in syrup, diced

You will need a 2 litre (3½ pint) ovenproof dish

1 Preheat the oven to Gas Mark 4/180°C/fan oven 160°C. Spray the ovenproof dish with the cooking spray.
2 Sift the flour and half the ground ginger into a large mixing bowl and stir in half the sugar.
3 Beat together the banana, milk, low fat spread and stem ginger, then stir into the flour until well combined. Spoon into the prepared dish.
4 In a saucepan, mix the remaining sugar and ground ginger with 150 ml (5 fl oz) water and bring to the boil. Pour this over the pudding then bake on a baking tray for 35–40 minutes until golden and springy to touch. Serve warm.

Date crunch

Calories per serving 152   Makes 12
15 mins prep, 30 mins cooking + 30 mins cooling

Semolina or dried polenta can be used in this recipe. It gives the shortbread-style mixture a lovely crunch.

low fat cooking spray
150 g (5½ oz) pitted dates
finely grated zest and juice of a lemon
125 g (4½ oz) self raising flour
125 g (4½ oz) semolina
75 g (2¾ oz) low fat spread
75 g (2¾ oz) light brown sugar

You will need an 18 cm (7 inch) square baking tin

1 Preheat the oven to Gas Mark 5/190°C/fan oven 170°C. Spray the baking tin with the cooking spray. Place the dates in a small pan with the lemon juice and 2 tablespoons of water. Simmer gently for 5 minutes until soft and mushy. Beat or mash to a smooth paste and set aside to cool.
2 Sift the flour into a mixing bowl and stir in the semolina.
3 Place the low fat spread and sugar in a small pan over a low heat and melt gently, then stir in the lemon zest. Pour over the flour and mix to a stiff dough. Press half of the dough into the tin. Spread the date mixture over the dough, then top with the remaining dough, pressing down gently. Bake for 30 minutes until golden.
4 Remove from the oven. Cut into squares. Leave to cool in the tin for about 30 minutes. Store in an airtight container for up to 5 days.

Pineapple muffins

Calories per serving 115   *Makes 12*
10 mins prep, 20 mins cooking

One of the easiest muffin recipes you'll find.

30 g (1¼ oz) low fat spread
200 g (7 oz) wholemeal self raising flour
1 teaspoon baking powder
1 teaspoon ground ginger
75 g (2¾ oz) light brown sugar
1 egg, beaten
432 g can crushed pineapple in natural juice,
    drained, reserving 100 ml (3½ fl oz) juice

You will need a 12 hole muffin tin; 12 muffin cases

1 Preheat the oven to Gas Mark 4/180°C/fan oven 160°C. Line the muffin tin with the muffin cases.
2 Place the low fat spread in a small saucepan over a low heat and melt. Place all the ingredients in a food processor and blend just briefly enough to combine the ingredients. Alternatively, sift the flour, baking powder and ginger into a large mixing bowl. Add the melted spread and the remaining ingredients, whisking until just combined.
3 Spoon into the paper cases and bake for 15–20 minutes. Cool on a wire rack.

Cherry and lime cupcakes

Calories per serving 127   *Makes 12*
15 mins prep, 20 mins cooking
 un-iced cakes only

Everyone enjoys a cupcake treat and these look especially pretty decorated with chopped cherries.

75 g (2¾ oz) low fat spread
100 g (3½ oz) caster sugar
2 eggs, beaten
½ teaspoon vanilla extract
100 g (3½ oz) self raising flour
finely grated zest and juice of a lime
60 g (2 oz) glacé cherries, quartered
40 g (1½ oz) icing sugar

You will need a 12 hole bun tray (smaller and shallower than a muffin tray); 12 fairy cake cases

1 Preheat the oven to Gas Mark 5/190°C/fan oven 170°C. Line the bun tray with the cake cases.
2 Place the low fat spread and caster sugar in a mixing bowl and beat until pale and creamy. Add the eggs a little at a time, whisking continuously, then whisk in the vanilla. Sift over the flour and fold in with the lime zest and two thirds of the cherries. Spoon the mixture into the paper cases and bake for 15–20 minutes until golden and springy to touch. Remove from the oven and transfer to a wire rack to cool.
3 Mix the icing sugar with 2–3 teaspoons of lime juice and spoon over the cakes. Slice the remaining cherries thinly and use to decorate the tops. Store in an airtight container for up to 3 days.

Muscovado and fig cake

Calories per serving 201   Serves 8

10 mins prep, 30 mins cooking + cooling

A lightly spiced, orange figgy cake with a lovely hint of muscovado sweetness.

juice and finely grated zest of an orange
125 g (4½ oz) ready to eat dried figs, chopped
175 g (6 oz) self raising flour
½ teaspoon baking powder
½ teaspoon cinnamon
½ teaspoon ground allspice
15 g (½ oz) ground almonds
100 g (3½ oz) dark muscovado sugar
30 g (1¼ oz) low fat spread, melted
2 eggs, beaten

You will need a 20 cm (8 inch) round tin; non stick baking parchment

1 Preheat the oven to Gas Mark 4/180°C/fan oven 160°C. Line the base of the tin with the baking parchment.

2 Put the orange juice into a measuring jug and make it up to 150 ml (5 fl oz) with water. Pour into a small pan and then add the figs. Bring to the boil and simmer gently for 3 minutes. Remove from the heat to cool.

3 Meanwhile, sift the flour, baking powder and spices into a large bowl. Mix in the ground almonds, sugar and orange zest. Stir the low fat spread into the eggs and then pour the mixture into the flour. Add the figs and orange juice. Combine and spoon into the tin. Bake for 30 minutes or until a skewer inserted comes out clean.

4 Cool in the tin for 10 minutes before turning out on to a wire rack to cool completely.

cook's tip...

This cake is even more delicious and moist the day after baking, so if you can resist it for that long, once cold, store in an airtight container for up to 5 days.

index